ON THE MEDIEVAL STRUCTURE OF SPIRITUALITY:
THOMAS AQUINAS

Past Light on Present Life:
Theology, Ethics, and Spirituality

Roger Haight, SJ, Alfred Pach III,
and *Amanda Avila Kaminski,* series editors

These volumes are offered to the academic community of teachers and learners in the fields of Christian history, theology, ethics, and spirituality. They introduce classic texts by authors whose contributions have markedly affected the development of Christianity, especially in the West. The texts are accompanied by an introductory essay on context and key themes and followed by an interpretation that dialogically engages the original message with the issues of ethics, theology, and spirituality in the present.

On the Medieval Structure of Spirituality

THOMAS AQUINAS

EDITED AND WITH COMMENTARY BY
Roger Haight, SJ, Alfred Pach III,
and *Amanda Avila Kaminski*

FORDHAM UNIVERSITY PRESS   NEW YORK 2022

This series has been generously supported by a
theological education grant from the E. Rhodes
and Leona B. Carpenter Foundation.

All selections are reprinted from *Summa Theologica,
Part I-II (Pars Prima Secundae)*, from the Complete
American Edition by Thomas Aquinas, translated by
Fathers of the English Dominican Province. Public domain.

Visit us online at www.fordhampress.com.

Library of Congress Control Number: 2022905131

Printed in the United States of America

24 23 22   5 4 3 2 1

First edition

Contents

ON THE MEDIEVAL STRUCTURE OF SPIRITUALITY:
THOMAS AQUINAS

I

Introduction to Thomas Aquinas and the Texts

One could make the case that Thomas Aquinas had more influence on the way Christians understand spirituality than any other human being after Jesus and Paul. Some would reserve that dignity to Augustine, but Aquinas was an Augustinian who incorporated Augustine's teachings in a new linguistic system. Thomas's language affected all Catholics after him and many Protestants who locate themselves for or against some of his basic concepts. He helped make Aristotelian concepts an integral part of theology; he tied our reflections on scriptural language to the scientific thinking of his time; he united faith and reason into a comprehensive synthesis; with his theology of grace he gave spirituality a new metaphysical grounding; he provided a basis for understanding how contemplation and action required each other and how one's action in the world united one to God. He did all this in abstract theological language where the term *abstract* has a double meaning. It refers to what became the technical language of the schools and universities as distinct from everyday discourse; but also instead of lifting a disembodied conceptual language out of reality, it focused insight

3

and enabled understanding to penetrate what is going on within the flow of sense data in the concrete narratives of living day-to-day.

Aquinas's students spent their university days speaking the language of the schools of the thirteenth century and of the texts preserved from earlier times. Because it was not a twentieth-century idiom, we need a thoroughgoing introduction to its context. Even a schematic approach to this complex period in Western European history has to notice some of the many ways in which it leapt into the renaissance beyond the early Middle Ages, drew the past up into a comprehensively different culture, and formulated a thoroughly new theology that remained remarkably continuous with the tradition. What follows simply marks some of the stages that must be recognized as the presuppositions of the textual witness. There we see the historical burgeoning of the High Middle Ages and a solidified Christendom. In 1224 or 1225 Thomas was born into that world in Aquino, a village between Rome and Naples set up in the mountains not far from Benedict's Monte Cassino Monastery. Early on, Thomas was headed for a university education. His writing reflects the new dynamism of learning that was mediated by the professionalization of the discipline of theology in the university and the use of Aristotelian language.[1]

As a consequence, this introduction follows a somewhat serpentine route to the texts presented in this volume. We begin with the renaissance in the High Middle Ages in Europe, the formation of the universities, and the jolt that the discovery of Aristotle gave to intellectual life. Thomas Aquinas is the child and a leading mediator of the transitions of this period. Understanding his work requires close attention to the new methods of learning that were occurring in the thirteenth century and the intellectual language that Aristotle provided. He introduced some basic ideas and terms that governed a more critical way of thinking. Only then can we turn to a brief explanation of the subject matter of these texts: Thomas's theology of grace, the nature and role of virtues in human life, and the idea of natural law that became so closely associated with Catholic spirituality. It should be clear that what Aquinas represents in these writings is a foundational map, a metaphysics, of the Christian life.

Europe, the University, and Aristotle

Thomas Aquinas wrote a massive synthesis that organized a Christian self-understanding into a genuine worldview. It became a standard for the theology of the schools. Some of its basic ideas live on and are taken for granted. But they first surfaced in a world as different from our own as Aquinas's was from Augustine's. The new Medieval culture cannot be represented in a few pages, but it has to be acknowledged; and the elementary concepts of the new Aristotelian language have to be described. In lieu of a history of Western Europe, what follows points to the economic, social, and cultural dynamisms of the eleventh and twelfth centuries, the new position of the church in Western Europe, and the influence of the university and Aristotle on theology during the thirteenth century.[2]

Europe and the church. The year 1000 can be used as an approximation of when many dimensions of cultural life began to converge into an extensive drift in Western Europe. More regional order meant it was easier to travel; increased travel energized commerce between regions; more business meant more wealth and development in town life. Church historians document an expansion and reform of monastic life as taking off in the tenth and eleventh centuries. The impact of monastic life often extended far beyond a renewal of piety; monasteries could stimulate agrarian development that in turn spawned the social life of an area.

So, too, a revival and reform of the order of monastic life can be correlated with a more serious understanding and practice of general ecclesiastical discipline. In 1049, when the Holy Roman Emperor Henry III intended to reform the papacy, he turned to the monasteries for a team of monks, outsiders relative to Roman ways, and committed the task to them. Over a period of decades, they gradually reasserted broader institutional authority of the church in Western Europe. The Gregorian Reform, named after Hildebrand who ascended to the papacy in 1073 after serving in other positions of leadership and took the name of Gregory VII, transformed the basic organization of the Western Roman Church. By establishing an administrative bureaucracy of cardinals and determining an internal and independent system of papal elections, the reformers established papal autonomy. They then expanded papal authority to distant cities with a system of delegates and enforced it by the threat of excommunication. By insisting on higher standards for ordination, including the discipline of celibacy, the reformers elevated the social and ecclesial role of priest-minister that would gradually develop into clericalism. The present polity of the Roman Catholic Church is still essentially "Gregorian"; in a way that is unique in Christianity, the term *church* refers to a massive universal institution.

Thirteenth-century Europe bore eloquent witness to the effects of the social renaissance and the Gregorian Reform. In 1215, Pope Innocent III presided over the Fourth Lateran Council, so called because it met in the Lateran Palace in Rome. It had widespread attendance and passed far-ranging legislation over all aspects of church life, from doctrine to discipline. It reflected an apogee of papal authority over an ecclesial presence that was felt in all aspects of life on the ground, even as the new Gothic spires could be seen from a distance in so many towns and small cities.

The university. Another soft date for the beginning of universities in Medieval Europe is 1200. There were many and some great theologians before that date, but theology was largely associated with monasteries or schools attached to episcopal churches. The setting was more or less enclosed, and the method of theology depended on authority, principally of the texts of the tradition. The university, by contrast, may be associated with urbanization, with the organization of distinct schools into unified systems, and a professionalization of learning into disciplines: law, medicine, philosophy, and theology. Latin served as a common language that united professors and students across cultures and actualized communication between regions. The universities, not independent from church authority, formed another bond that helped to unite Western Europe.

The university also had a direct and important effect on the discipline of theology. The setting had changed: from the monastery or small school to the city with a larger and more diverse set of professors and students. The theology of the university had a formal task to perform: "to teach theology . . . in fixed-time degree courses offering a portable set of skills to be used by the Church's priesthood in the liturgical, pastoral, and homiletic service of the Church."[3]

Aristotle and theology. As universities were being formed in various cities in Europe, other centers were discovering the works of Aristotle largely through Muslim sources and commentators. Teams in Spain and Southern Italy were dedicated to translating Aristotle's logic, his natural philosophy, and his metaphysics into Latin. Aristotle was an empiricist. If Plato looked to heavenly ideas to explain the world's order, Aristotle observed the actual order of earthly exchange. A Platonic tradition indirectly influenced Augustine's thinking; his theological method consisted of commentary on the texts of the tradition. The drift of Aristotle's empirical and objective thinking gradually introduced a distinctly new way of understanding the symbols of Christian faith and unleashed deep tensions in theological learning. A couple of themes in this tension are crucial for understanding the import of Aquinas's teaching and the texts presented here.

The first point regards Aristotle's suppositions and style of thinking. As an empiricist he worked with what he observed. As will be discussed more fully below, Aristotle perceived that each kind of being, we might say species, has an internal nature that determines how it behaves. The stress in this idea falls on the phrase *internal nature*: the nature of a thing is its intrinsic character. In it one finds the reason or inner logic for behavior of everything inside creation itself and within each kind of being. External forces do not explain actions; they depend on an inner wiring. Therefore, if one wants to understand something, one does not appeal to outside reasons or heavenly ideas, but to an inner principle or rationale. This shifts attention in understanding from texts to empirical scrutiny, and, more deeply, from completely relying on authority to looking for the inner proclivities that explain behavior.

The second point is analogous but pushes further and runs more deeply. Monastic theology kept the authoritative tradition alive and relevant by commentary. Its contemplative character correlated more easily with a rural setting. Aristotle's thinking was driven by a critical investigative spirit. Why does the tradition say what it does? and How does one resolve contradictory opinions in the same authoritative tradition? Aristotle's logic offered syllogistically clear thinking. For example, if A equals B, and one finds that B also equals C, then C too is equal to A. Also, Aristotle's metaphysical categories of form and matter, and his view of different patterns of how causality operates, provided a formal diagram of the inner elements and working of all things. These were used as a way of addressing and understanding everything with consistent rational precision.

Something analogous to nineteenth-century science and twentieth-century "secularization" was unleashed by Aristotle's thinking but in a most subtle and highly intellectual way. The process differs from what Clement of Alexandria accomplished.[4] He saw Greek philosophy as inspired by the Word of God with imagined links to early Hebrew thinking. Aristotle, by contrast, inspired new thoughts for Aquinas. First, one can distinguish between faith and reason without predicating hostility between them; they are two paths to one truth. He distinguished them to know how they fitted together. Second, we see a strong confidence in the power of reason coupled with the authority of the tradition. The number of questions Aquinas asked and answered in his two *Summas* is astonishing. Third, these two factors congealed into a spirit of theological enthusiasm, a corporate sense that theological investigation was entering a new phase beyond commentary on received texts. Old topics were subjected to new questions, opinions were debated, and conclusions were drawn on the basis of reason.

Thomas Aquinas

We have gotten ahead of ourselves because, while these currents in theology were running throughout the thirteenth century, Thomas Aquinas himself was one of their most influential agents. As noted earlier, he was born in 1224 or 1225 in Aquino, not far from Benedict's monastery, and he received his first education with the monks.

At around the age of fifteen Aquinas was sent to the recently founded university in Naples. At that time texts of Aristotle were being discovered and translated from Islamic sources and "were beginning to make their way through Naples into Europe."[5] He also met some Dominicans there. Domingo de Guzman had founded the band of preachers in the early thirteenth century, and it gained papal approval in 1216. Like the Franciscans, the Dominicans' charism replaced monastic enclosure and stability with mobility. The new Order of Preachers essentially consisted of mendicant preachers who were at home in towns and cities and trained in houses of study at the universities.

"In April 1244, Thomas Aquinas stunned his parents and family by taking the habit of the Dominican order from the hands of the prior in Naples."[6] He was nineteen or twenty years old. It is generally thought that Thomas's family believed that he would become a Benedictine monk; it was an established way of life. In any case, when his family learned of his commitment to the Dominicans they in effect kidnapped him and brought him home to think about it for a year before he had his way.

The next phase of Aquinas's education, from 1245 to 1256, transpired in Paris and Cologne during which time he was mentored by Albert the Great, a Dominican well-versed in the work of Aristotle. He finished his extensive commentary on the Sentences of Peter Lombard in Paris.[7] This was the standard resource for theology at the time, and he was declared a master of theology in 1256. The rest of Aquinas's life was that of a scholar who spent his time studying Aristotle, writing, and teaching students, especially in Dominican houses of study. He left Paris in 1259 and spent time in Naples, Orvieto, and Rome. While at Rome teaching at a Dominican house of studies, Aquinas began work on his *Summa Theologiae* in 1265. "What sparked the composition of the *Summa Theologiae* was a very specific request by his superiors to undertake the wholesale reform of Dominican theological education."[8] With it, Aquinas transformed theology into a discipline: a subject matter with its sources and a specific method to generate understanding that contrasted with monastic theology.

Aquinas returned for another residency at the University of Paris from 1269 to 1272, when he moved to Naples to establish a new Dominican house of studies. He ceased working late in 1273 and died in March of 1274 en route to the General Council held in Lyons that year.

The Scholastic Form of Aquinas's *Summa Theologiae*

The texts of Aquinas contained in this volume are drawn from his signature work, *Summa Theologiae*, or what he called "sacred doctrine," a summary compilation of Christian beliefs and responses to theological questions. While the form of this massive four-volume work seems to be distinctive, it mimics educational patterns of learning in the schools.[9] Professors learned by extensive historical study of the subject matter across historical anthologies or preserved texts. For the most part they communicated their learning to the students through lecture and note-taking. But they also pushed the boundaries of accepted doctrine, especially when the tradition failed to present a common opinion. When an issue was considered, and the authoritative witnesses offered a split decision, which one was true? Frequently professors would publicly address an issue by posing a precise question to the tradition, reviewing the historical responses both for and against an opinion, and resolving the issue by reasoning from commonly accepted principles. This gave the theologian leverage to declare some opinions mistaken and others closer to the truth. By examining what is going on in this exercise one can discern a new confidence in reason's ability to consider the evidences of past witnesses and draw new conclusions that were faithful to the past and reasonable in the present.

Thomas Aquinas's *Summa Theologiae* has a grand architectural design that resembles a neo-Platonic depiction of reality that comes forth from God and then returns to God; in the Christian view, this is mediated through Jesus Christ. Inside this massive metaphysical framework, Aquinas locates human beings as knowers and moral agents helped by God's grace along the way of life: coming from and returning to God. Within that large framework, the text of the *Summa* is divided into parts and subdivided into treatises on specific subject matters. But the most basic units of the whole of the *Summa* remain the short "articles" that imitate a probing discussion such as the one just described. Thomas picks a precise issue, asks a question, gives opposing sides from the tradition, responds to the question in a reasoned way often from an acknowledged principle, and resolves the opposing views. These articles are the building stones of this massive medieval cathedral of thought.

Basic Categories in Thomas Aquinas

Before introducing the texts that present key elements in the spiritual life of the Christian, we turn to a description of a few basic concepts drawn by Aquinas from Aristotle in his analyses of human existence. These represent a fundamental orientation to his thinking, explain some of his essential vocabulary, and describe the place of human existence within the whole of reality. In effect, this overview amounts to an essential glossary.

Natures. The world is composed of many different kinds of beings, and each being is determined by its nature. The term *nature* has several but two principal functions: it characterizes the identity or kind of being any particular thing is, and it is the principle or reason for its acting the way it does. For example, a tree is a tree, or a particular kind of tree, because of its inner constituent nature; and it behaves the way it does for the same reason. While all this seems to be no more than the definition of terms, looking at natures as sources of operation and action gives a dynamic slant to appreciating the world. These natures interact with each other and form a massive organism of moving parts.

Powers. Things act the way they do because they have the power to do so. Take for example human beings. Humans can understand things and can make decisions because they have the powers to do so: an intellect with which to think and a will as an ability to choose and decide. Metaphysical law says that every act requires an ability to perform it. Human nature has built into it the powers of intellect and will that enable understanding, reflecting, deciding, and acting in a self-conscious way.[10]

Habits and Virtues. The term *habit* refers to a modification, or quality, or groove that affects a power and enables it to do what it does easily and even instinctively. All people are familiar with the habits that they develop: "I've trained myself to do this or that automatically." One builds up a habit by exercise. Although we can isolate major personal habits that govern our lives, the category also refers to spheres of human dispositions that govern important sets of responses to reality. A virtue essentially is a good habit: it leans us toward spontaneously performing morally good actions.

Actions. The idea of an action almost goes without saying; it is self-evident. But the point in Aquinas's system lies in actions that flow from natures and powers and virtues. Natures determine all the actions of specific finite beings; each being acts according to its nature as distinct from another nature.

Coherence and integrity to the whole. The idea *integrity* moves to a higher level of abstraction and generalization but lies buried in the earlier definitions. Coherence, integrity, and correspondence characterize the relationship between natures, powers, virtues, and actions. This particular action belongs to this kind or nature of being that is equipped with this or that power to do what it needs to do to be itself. Once again, this seems like no more than common sense analysis to our ears; and so it is. But Aquinas, by borrowing the terms from Aristotle, has fashioned these ideas into linguistic instruments for clear thinking. Like the definitions of terms in a dictionary provide the elemental tools for consistent, communicable, and creative thinking, the elements of nature and action allow for clear analysis of the processes of actual beings.

Teleology. Teleology refers abstractly to the way systems of actions function as means and are directed toward a goal. *Telos* is Greek, referring to the "end" or "goal" of something. Sometimes this means no more than each part or action contributes to a whole; the rationale for legs lies in their organic relation to a system of locomotion. Sometimes teleology has a meaning rooted in intentionality, as in people performing actions toward an intended goal. Aristotle thought pervasively in terms of means and ends because teleology seemed to offer such an obvious explanation of things: the reason for things lay in their function, what they were for.

Proportionality. A last abstract characteristic of the system contains a vital ingredient in Aquinas's view of reality and provides a key to his Christian spirituality. A proportional fit or correspondence in character exists between the functions of nature, powers, actions, and the goal to which they are aimed or fitted. There is a line of likeness that stretches from nature to goal, one that basically stands to organic reason. If anthropologists find tools in an ancient grave site, they take it to reflect the nature of the hominid.

This principle becomes vitally important in one's overall assessment of the human person. Like Aristotle, Aquinas held that all beings were teleologically oriented toward their fulfillment or happiness. So too human beings. The answer to the question of the goal of human existence or what constitutes human fulfillment corresponds with human nature. The orientation of human nature to its ultimate goal also provides the grounding of all spirituality, understood as the way people live in relation to what they deem their ultimate end. Aquinas's teleological structure of spirituality responds to these basic questions: Who am I? Why am I here? Where am I going? And how do I get there? Like all other beings, humans have a nature, fitted to a goal, and all of them get there by exercising their powers, modified by virtues in actions.

We can conclude this glossary with a simple formula that offers a framework for reading Aquinas's theological metaphysics for spirituality. Proportionality governs the dynamics of teleology, so that specific natures → have specific powers → qualified by various virtues → that elicit proportionate acts → that lead actors to their proper goal. In the case of human beings, we have rational natures, blessed with the powers of intellect and will, that, when graced with the virtues of faith, hope, and love, tend to elicit actions according to those virtues in a life-long process that leads to the goal of life with God. All human beings come from God and are meant to return to God.

The Texts

The spirituality contained in the writings of Thomas Aquinas embodies a comprehensive worldview with very definite contours that are quite different from our own modern, secular, scientific, and evolutionary view of reality. The texts contained in this volume rapidly lead us from that macro vision to a granular view of Aquinas on grace and the virtues. One more prenote is required to ease the passage from abstract worldview to commonsensical description: the role of grace as a new human nature.

Thomas Aquinas still lived in Augustine's Christian world that recognized sin as a pervasive force in human life. No one could achieve salvation on their own; salvation intrinsically depended on God's grace. Aquinas recognized a human ability to perform good human acts like planting fields and harvesting crops, but human beings have been called to a higher personal union with God. Human fulfillment so conceived absolutely exceeded innate human power and was possible only on the basis of God's active help: grace. In effect, because of the disproportionality of human nature and its powers to the supernatural goal to which it has been called, human beings require a "new nature" proportional to that supernatural goal. Most fundamentally, in terms of Aquinas's systemic thinking, the primary meaning of the term grace is the transformed "nature" that is supplied to human beings so that they can reach their eternal goal, with new powers or virtues won for them by Jesus Christ.[11] In Aquinas's time the Augustinian supposition still prevailed that, because of the fallen nature of human beings, everyone did not share in this economy of grace.

A sympathetic appropriation of the language of Aquinas in a way that makes sense in our day requires interpretation. It has to avoid the tendency to think in mechanistic terms and actively translate the language in terms of existential life. Aquinas also had a limited worldview and was not pointedly addressing the religious pluralism that surrounds us today. His theology of grace presupposes human beings consciously living inside Christian churches, which assembled and received sacraments, rather than addressing how grace might work outside the Christian sphere. A positive interpretation of Aquinas on grace, virtue and the spiritual life will focus on existential life within the Christian sphere before looking for its universal applicability.

We begin the introduction to the texts on grace and then the virtues with the supposition that Aquinas is working his way through an account of how Christians are able to guide their lives in their journey to final union with God, which constitutes ultimate salvation. Grace in effect supplies a human being with a principle of operation that supports such a life. Aquinas communicates this large view by responding to a series of questions.

On grace. What is grace? Grace denotes, first of all, a kind of being that, when received, becomes inherent in the human soul. In Thomistic language this refers to a quality or disposition or characteristic of the soul.[12] Rather than a virtue that modifies a human power, it qualifies the spiritual self. Only God can be the author of God's grace. Grace is the effect in the human spirit of God's presence sustaining it within a person. It flows from God's positive love of human beings.

God's grace effects forgiveness of sin and justifies a human person. An analysis of Aquinas's discussion of this "question" (ST I-II, q.113, a.1) reveals the process of inculturation of biblical language into the new Aristotelian language of the university. Aquinas begins by citing Paul on justification and gradually he slides into more philosophical and theological terms.

Aquinas also brings up the question of merit: can a person really merit anything from God? His answer to this question, which says yes, really means no: such is its subtlety. Aquinas presupposes that God's grace is prior to any positive human response to God, which is in turn supported by grace in the doing; and that support continues in human perseverance. Despite this, Aquinas says we can talk about a certain kind of merit in the sense that justification does not happen outside of human freedom, but within it. His speech about merit is thus misleading because grace is the precondition of all salvific human response to God: we cannot gain merit on our own, but we can with God's grace.

On virtue. Virtues essentially consist of habits that influence human powers. For example, acuity in mathematics might be a virtue that is built up in the intellect by continual practice or study. Of course, a virtue is a good habit and a vice is a bad habit. Aquinas responds to four questions to build this basic understanding because there were other current conceptions of virtue in play. But of special note relative to spirituality are the *theological* virtues of faith, hope, and charity. Aquinas calls these "infused" virtues because they cannot be manufactured by human practice but can only be given as divine gifts that accompany the gift of grace itself. Faith dwells in the intellect and charity dwells in the will, while hope dwells in the intellect but flows through other virtues like courage into willing and acting consistently.

What is distinctive about these theological virtues lies in their provenance; they cannot be generated by moral practice but are the gifts that accompany grace. This shows how grace raises the whole human system of response, nature-powers-dispositions-actions, into a "higher" or divinely suffused and assisted sphere of operation, one that is consistent and pro-portionate with the divine goal for human existence, personal union with God.[13]

Added to the selections of Aquinas on the virtues are some questions on natural law and how this so-called natural law relates to a moral life. This bears some importance because Aquinas's virtue ethics are often contrasted with ethics based on law, and the tradition of the ten commandments which deeply influences Christian spirituality. To begin, a law is not a habit or a virtue; a law is a precept or command that sometimes comes from outside the self and sometimes from within. Natural law, rather than being a series of precepts, refers more generally to the right order of things; it does not consist of many laws but of a few basic principles like "do good and avoid evil." This sphere, ultimately grounded in the consistency of the interrelated actions of natures, in turn grounds all moral behavior. Thus, all acts of virtue are somehow included in these basic rational and moral principles that reflect the order of the world. These principles are so all-encompassing that they cannot be changed because they reflect the very structure of reality and all people can call them to consciousness. The key to natural law, then, resides in the human mind that always seeks the grounds of morality in reality itself.

On spirituality as action. As Denys Turner notices, Thomas Aquinas disappears in his writing behind the subject matter.[14] The Aristotelian analysis leaves little room for the passion or emotion of the author. But the flood of light he throws on the life of the human subject stimulates a kind of intellectual pleasure. Aquinas supplies a map for a spirituality that encompasses the whole active life of a person. These texts cannot replicate the energy and power of the whole *Summa Theologiae,* but they schematize the whole of a person's life in a temporal continuum of reflection and action. That spiritual process comes from God and, raised up through grace to a new level of operation, it embraces all one's actions and leads a person toward eternal life.

Notes

1. Aquinas "reconceives theology as a teachable, examinable, portable, intellectual skill; he disengages the practice of theology

from its enclosure within the secluded and specifically prayerful practices of the cloister, liberating it for a multitasking practice in the street." Denys Turner, *Thomas Aquinas: A Portrait* (New Haven: Yale University Press, 2013), 33.

2. M.-D. Chenu represents the context of Aquinas's work in *Toward Understanding Saint Thomas*, trans. A.-M. Landry and D. Hughes (Chicago: Henry Regnery, 1964), 11–78.

3. Turner, *Thomas Aquinas*: 23.

4. See *Enculturating Christian Spirituality: Clement of Alexandria* (New York: Fordham University Press, 2023).

5. Herbert McCabe, *On Aquinas*, ed. Brian Davies (London: Burns & Oates, 2008), 2.

6. Turner, *Thomas Aquinas*, 8.

7. The Sentences of Peter Lombard were a collection of texts and opinions of particularly the Fathers of the church collected in the mid-twelfth century and revised into four books divided topically in the thirteenth century.

8. Turner, *Thomas Aquinas*, 25.

9. Chenu traces the evolution of the literary form of Aquinas's *Summa Theologiae* in *Toward Understanding Saint Thomas*, 79–99.

10. One cannot separate intellect and will. They are not two powers side-by-side but mutually inform each other. "There is no act of practical intelligence which is not also one of will, and vice versa." McCabe, *On Aquinas*, 68.

11. This is a qualified judgment that is open to further interpretation. It is difficult to interpret Thomas Aquinas reductively because of the richness of the totality of his thought. Later dynamic and existentialist interpretations of Aquinas's thought can qualify and nuance this straightforward equation of grace with being a new nature. It is most important here to recognize that "nature" does not primarily mean an "essence" or "kind of being" at this point but is a dynamic principle of activity.

12. Grace is a form of being but not a substantial being or thing in itself; it is rather a quality of a being, like its motion, color, relationships, position, and so on. Aristotle called these characteristics of a substance "accidents."

13. Everything is rooted in God and God's grace; the infused theological virtues form a basis for Aquinas's understanding of

Christian spirituality, primarily the love of God for us that can be correlated with grace. "This divine charity of ours, says Aquinas, is first of all our response to God's love for us. So first there is mutual love which makes us friends with God, sharing in his life and joy. This is the foundation of Christian morality: not a code of conduct but our friendship with God, or sharing in his Spirit, which shows itself in our love for God's friends and creatures." Herbert McCabe, *Faith within Reason*, ed. Brian Davies (London: Continuum, 2007), 107.

14. Turner, *Thomas Aquinas*, 39.

II
The Texts

On Grace [ST I–II, Questions 110, 112, 113 and 114]

Question 110

Of the Grace of God as Regards Its Essence
(In Four Articles)

We must now consider the grace of God as regards its essence; and under this head there are four points of inquiry:

(1) Whether grace implies something in the soul?
(2) Whether grace is a quality?
(3) Whether grace differs from infused virtue?
(4) Of the subject of grace.

First Article [I–II, Q. 110, Art. 1]

Whether Grace Implies Anything in the Soul?

Objection 1: It would seem that grace does not imply anything in the soul. For man is said to have the grace of God even as the grace of man. Hence it is written (Gen. 39:21) that the Lord gave to Joseph "grace [Douay: 'favor'] in the sight of the chief keeper of the prison." Now when we say that a man has the favor of another, nothing is implied in him who has the favor of the other, but an acceptance is implied in him whose favor he has. Hence when we say that a man has the grace of God, nothing is implied in his soul; but we merely signify the Divine acceptance.

Obj. 2: Further, as the soul quickens the body so does God quicken the soul; hence it is written (Deut. 30:20): "He is thy life." Now the soul quickens the body immediately. Therefore nothing can come as a medium between God and the soul. Hence grace implies nothing created in the soul.

Obj. 3: Further, on Rom. 1:7, "Grace to you and peace," the gloss says: "Grace, i.e. the remission of sins." Now the remission of sin implies nothing in the soul, but only in God, Who does not impute the sin, according to Ps. 31:2: "Blessed is the man to whom the Lord hath not imputed sin." Hence neither does grace imply anything in the soul.

On the contrary, Light implies something in what is enlightened. But grace is a light of the soul; hence Augustine says (De Natura et Gratia xxii): "The light of truth rightly deserts the prevaricator of the law, and those who have been thus deserted become blind." Therefore grace implies something in the soul.

I answer that, According to the common manner of speech, grace is usually taken in three ways. First, for anyone's love, as we are accustomed to say that the soldier is in the good graces of the king, i.e. the king looks on him with favor. Secondly, it is taken for any gift freely bestowed, as we are accustomed to say: I do you this act of grace. Thirdly, it is taken for the recompense of a gift given "gratis," inasmuch as we are said to be "grateful" for benefits. Of these three the second depends on the first, since one bestows something on another "gratis" from the love wherewith he receives him into his good "graces." And from the second proceeds the third, since from benefits bestowed "gratis" arises "gratitude."

Now as regards the last two, it is clear that grace implies something in him who receives grace: first, the gift given gratis; secondly, the acknowledgment of the gift. But as regards the first, a difference must be noted between the grace of God and the grace of man; for since the creature's good springs from the Divine will, some good in the creature flows from God's love, whereby He wishes the good of the creature. On the other hand, the will of man is moved by the good preexisting in things; and hence man's love does not wholly cause the good of the thing, but presupposes it either in part or wholly. Therefore it is clear that every love of God is followed at some time by a good caused in the creature, but not co-eternal with the eternal love. And according to this difference of good the love of God to the creature is looked at differently. For one is common, whereby He loves "all things that are" (Wis. 11:25), and thereby gives things their natural being. But the second is a special love, whereby He draws the rational creature above the condition of its nature to a participation of the Divine good; and according to this love He is said to love anyone simply, since it is by this love that God simply wishes the eternal good, which is Himself, for the creature.

Accordingly when a man is said to have the grace of God, there is signified something bestowed on man by God. Nevertheless the grace of God sometimes signifies God's eternal love, as we say the grace of predestination, inasmuch as God gratuitously and not from merits predestines or elects some; for it is written (Eph. 1:5): "He hath predestinated us into the adoption of children . . . unto the praise of the glory of His grace."

Reply Obj. 1: Even when a man is said to be in another's good graces, it is understood that there is something in him pleasing to the other; even as anyone is said to have God's grace—with this difference, that what is pleasing to a man in another is presupposed to his love, but whatever is pleasing to God in a man is caused by the Divine love, as was said above.

Reply Obj. 2: God is the life of the soul after the manner of an efficient cause; but the soul is the life of the body after the manner of a formal cause. Now there is no medium between form and matter, since the form, of itself, *informs* the matter or subject; whereas the agent *informs* the subject, not by its substance, but by the form, which it causes in the matter.

Reply Obj. 3: Augustine says (Retract. i, 25): "When I said that grace was for the remission of sins, and peace for our reconciliation with God, you must not take it to mean that peace and reconciliation do not pertain to general peace, but that the special name of grace signifies the remission of sins." Not only grace, therefore, but many other of God's gifts pertain to grace. And hence the remission of sins does not take place without some effect divinely caused in us, as will appear later (Q. 113, A. 2).

Second Article [I–II, Q. 110, Art. 2]

Whether Grace Is a Quality of the Soul?

Objection 1: It would seem that grace is not a quality of the soul. For no quality acts on its subject, since the action of a quality is not without the action of its subject, and thus the subject would necessarily act upon itself. But grace acts upon the soul, by justifying it. Therefore grace is not a quality.

Obj. 2: Furthermore, substance is nobler than quality. But grace is nobler than the nature of the soul, since we can do many things by grace, to which nature is not equal, as stated above (Q. 109, AA. 1, 2, 3). Therefore grace is not a quality.

Obj. 3: Furthermore, no quality remains after it has ceased to be in its subject. But grace remains; since it is not corrupted, for thus it would be reduced to nothing, since it was created from nothing; hence it is called a "new creature" (Gal. 6:15).

On the contrary, on Ps. 103:15: "That he may make the face cheerful with oil"; the gloss says: "Grace is a certain beauty of soul, which wins the Divine love." But beauty of soul is a quality, even as beauty of body. Therefore grace is a quality.

I answer that, As stated above (A. 1), there is understood to be an effect of God's gratuitous will in whoever is said to have God's grace. Now it was stated (Q. 109, A. 1) that man is aided by God's gratuitous will in two ways: first, inasmuch as man's soul is moved by God to know or will or do something, and in this way the gratuitous effect in man is not a quality, but a movement of the soul; for "motion is the act of the mover in the moved." Secondly, man is helped by God's gratuitous will, inasmuch as a habitual gift is infused by God into the soul; and for this reason, that it is not fitting that God should provide less for those He loves, that they may acquire supernatural good, than for creatures, whom He loves that they may acquire natural good. Now He so provides for natural creatures, that not merely does He move them to their natural acts, but He bestows upon them certain forms and powers, which are the principles of acts, in order that they may of themselves be inclined to these movements, and thus the movements whereby they are moved by God become natural and easy to creatures, according to Wis. 8:1: "she . . . ordereth all things sweetly." Much more therefore does He infuse into such as He moves towards the acquisition of supernatural good, certain forms or supernatural qualities, whereby they may be moved by Him sweetly and promptly to acquire eternal good; and thus the gift of grace is a quality.

Reply Obj. 1: Grace, as a quality, is said to act upon the soul, not after the manner of an efficient cause, but after the manner of a formal cause, as whiteness makes a thing white, and justice, just.

Reply Obj. 2: Every substance is either the nature of the thing whereof it is the substance or is a part of the nature, even as matter and form are called substance. And because grace is above human nature, it cannot be a substance or a substantial form, but is an accidental form of the soul. Now what is substantially in God, becomes accidental in the soul participating the Divine goodness, as is clear in the case of knowledge. And thus because the soul participates in the Divine goodness imperfectly, the participation of the Divine goodness, which is grace, has its being in the soul in a less perfect way than the soul subsists in itself. Nevertheless, inasmuch as it is the expression or participation of the Divine goodness, it is nobler than the nature of the soul, though not in its mode of being.

Reply Obj. 3: As Boethius [*Pseudo-Bede, Sent. Phil. ex Artist.] says, the "being of an accident is to inhere." Hence no accident is called being as if it had being, but because by it something is; hence it is said to belong to a being rather than to be a being (Metaph. vii, text. 2). And because to become and to be corrupted belong to what is, properly speaking, no accident comes into being or is corrupted, but is said to come into being and to be corrupted inasmuch as its subject begins or ceases to be in act with this accident. And thus grace is said to be created inasmuch as men are created with reference to it, i.e. are given a new being out of nothing, i.e. not from merits, according to Eph. 2:10, "created in Jesus Christ in good works."

Third Article [I–II, Q. 110, Art. 3]

Whether Grace Is the Same as Virtue?

Objection 1: It would seem that grace is the same as virtue. For Augustine says (De Spir. et Lit. xiv) that "operating grace is faith that worketh by charity." But faith that worketh by charity is a virtue. Therefore grace is a virtue.

Obj. 2: Further, what fits the definition, fits the defined. But the definitions of virtue given by saints and philosophers fit grace, since "it makes its subject good, and his work good," and "it is a good quality of the mind, whereby we live righteously," etc. Therefore grace is virtue.

Obj. 3: Further, grace is a quality. Now it is clearly not in the *fourth* species of quality; viz. *form* which is the "abiding figure of things," since it does not belong to bodies. Nor is it in the *third*, since it is not a "passion nor a passion-like quality," which is in the sensitive part of the soul, as is proved in *Physic.* viii; and grace is principally in the mind. Nor is it in the *second* species, which is "natural power" or "impotence"; since grace is above nature and does not regard good and evil, as does natural power. Therefore it must be in the *first* species which is "habit" or "disposition." Now habits of the mind are virtues; since even knowledge itself is a virtue after a manner, as stated above (Q. 57, AA. 1, 2). Therefore grace is the same as virtue.

On the contrary, If grace is a virtue, it would seem before all to be one of the three theological virtues. But grace is neither faith nor hope, for these can be without sanctifying grace. Nor is it charity, since "grace foreruns charity," as Augustine says in his book on the *Predestination of the Saints* (De Dono Persev. xvi). Therefore grace is not virtue.

I answer that, Some held that grace and virtue were identical in essence, and differed only logically—in the sense that we speak of grace inasmuch as it makes man pleasing to God, or is given gratuitously—and of virtue inasmuch as it empowers us to act rightly. And the Master seems to have thought this (Sent. ii, D 27).

But if anyone rightly considers the nature of virtue, this cannot hold, since, as the Philosopher says (Physic. vii, text. 17), "Virtue is disposition of what is perfect—and I call perfect what is disposed according to its nature." Now from this it is clear that the virtue of a thing has reference to some pre-existing nature, from the fact that everything is disposed with reference to what befits its nature. But it is manifest that the virtues acquired by human acts of which we spoke above (Q. 55, seqq.) are dispositions, whereby a man is fittingly disposed with reference to the nature whereby he is a man; whereas infused virtues dispose man in a higher manner and towards a higher end, and consequently in relation to some higher nature, i.e. in relation to a participation of the Divine Nature, according to 2 Pet. 1:4: "He hath given us most great and most precious promises; that by these you may be made partakers of the Divine Nature." And it is in respect of receiving this nature that we are said to be born again sons of God.

And thus, even as the natural light of reason is something besides the acquired virtues, which are ordained to this natural light, so also the light of grace which is a participation of the Divine Nature is something besides the infused virtues which are derived from and are ordained to this light, hence the Apostle says (Eph. 5:8): "For you were heretofore darkness, but now light in the Lord. Walk then as children of the light." For as the acquired virtues enable a man to walk, in accordance with the natural light of reason, so do the infused virtues enable a man to walk as befits the light of grace.

Reply Obj. 1: Augustine calls "faith that worketh by charity" grace, since the act of faith of him that worketh by charity is the first act by which sanctifying grace is manifested.

Reply Obj. 2: Good is placed in the definition of virtue with reference to its fitness with some pre-existing nature essential or participated. Now good is not attributed to grace in this manner, but as to the root of goodness in man, as stated above.

Reply Obj. 3: Grace is reduced to the first species of quality; and yet it is not the same as virtue, but is a certain disposition which is presupposed to the infused virtues, as their principle and root.

Fourth Article [I–II, Q. 110, Art. 4]

Whether Grace Is in the Essence of the Soul as in a Subject, or in One of the Powers?

Objection 1: It would seem that grace is not in the essence of the soul, as in a subject, but in one of the powers. For Augustine says (Hypognosticon iii [*Among the spurious

works of St. Augustine]) that grace is related to the will or to
the free will "as a rider to his horse." Now the will or the free
will is a power, as stated above (I, Q. 83, A. 2). Hence grace
is in a power of the soul, as in a subject.

Obj. 2: Further, "Man's merit springs from grace" as Augustine says (De Gratia et Lib. Arbit. vi). Now merit consists
in acts, which proceed from a power. Hence it seems that
grace is a perfection of a power of the soul.

Obj. 3: Further, if the essence of the soul is the proper
subject of grace, the soul, inasmuch as it has an essence, must
be capable of grace. But this is false; since it would follow
that every soul would be capable of grace. Therefore the essence of the soul is not the proper subject of grace.

Obj. 4: Further, the essence of the soul is prior to its powers.
Now what is prior may be understood without what is pos-
terior. Hence it follows that grace may be taken to be in the
soul, although we suppose no part or power of the soul—viz.
neither the will, nor the intellect, nor anything else; which is
impossible.

On the contrary, By grace we are born again sons of God.
But generation terminates at the essence prior to the powers.
Therefore grace is in the soul's essence prior to being in the
powers.

I answer that, This question depends on the preceding. For
if grace is the same as virtue, it must necessarily be in the
powers of the soul as in a subject; since the soul's powers are
the proper subject of virtue, as stated above (Q. 56, A. 1). But
if grace differs from virtue, it cannot be said that a power of
the soul is the subject of grace, since every perfection of the
soul's powers has the nature of virtue, as stated above (Q. 55,
A. 1; Q. 56, A. 1). Hence it remains that grace, as it is prior
to virtue, has a subject prior to the powers of the soul, so
that it is in the essence of the soul. For as man in his intellective powers participates in the Divine knowledge through
the virtue of faith, and in his power of will participates in the
Divine love through the virtue of charity, so also in the nature
of the soul does he participate in the Divine Nature, after the

manner of a likeness, through a certain regeneration or re-creation.

Reply Obj. 1: As from the essence of the soul flows its powers, which are the principles of deeds, so likewise the virtues, whereby the powers are moved to act, flow into the powers of the soul from grace. And thus grace is compared to the will as the mover to the moved, which is the same comparison as that of a horseman to the horse—but not as an accident to a subject.

And thereby is made clear the Reply to the Second Objection. For grace is the principle of meritorious works through the medium of virtues, as the essence of the soul is the principal of vital deeds through the medium of the powers.

Reply Obj. 3: The soul is the subject of grace, as being in the species of intellectual or rational nature. But the soul is not classed in a species by any of its powers, since the powers are natural properties of the soul following upon the species. Hence the soul differs specifically in its essence from other souls, viz. of dumb animals, and of plants. Consequently it does not follow that, if the essence of the human soul is the subject of grace, every soul may be the subject of grace; since it belongs to the essence of the soul, inasmuch as it is of such a species.

Reply Obj. 4: Since the powers of the soul are natural properties following upon the species, the soul cannot be without them. Yet, granted that it was without them, the soul would still be called intellectual or rational in its species, not that it would actually have these powers, but on account of the essence of such a species, from which these powers naturally flow.

Question 111

Of the Division of Grace

We must now consider the division of grace; under which head there are five points of inquiry [two of which are reproduced here]:

(1) Whether grace is fittingly divided into gratuitous grace and sanctifying grace?

(2) Of the division into operating and cooperating grace;

First Article [I–I, Q. 111, A 1]

Whether grace is fittingly divided into sanctifying grace and gratuitous grace?

Objection 1: It would seem that grace is not fittingly divided into sanctifying grace and gratuitous grace. For grace is a gift of God, as is clear from what has been already stated (Question [110], Article [1]). But man is not therefore pleasing to God because something is given him by God, but rather on the contrary; since something is freely given by God, because man is pleasing to Him. Hence there is no sanctifying grace.

Obj. 2: Further, whatever is not given on account of preceding merits is given gratis. Now even natural good is given to man without preceding merit, since nature is presupposed to merit.

Therefore nature itself is given gratuitously by God. But nature is condivided with grace. Therefore to be gratuitously given is not fittingly set down as a difference of grace, since it is found outside the genus of grace.

Obj. 3: Further, members of a division are mutually opposed. But even sanctifying grace, whereby we are justified, is given to us gratuitously, according to Rm. 3:24: "Being justified freely [gratis] by His grace." Hence sanctifying grace ought not to be divided against gratuitous grace.

On the contrary, The Apostle attributes both to grace, viz. to sanctify and to be gratuitously given. For with regard to the first he says (Eph. 1:6): "He hath graced us in His beloved son." And with regard to the second (Rm. 2:6): "And if by grace, it is not now by works, otherwise grace is no more grace." Therefore grace can be distinguished by its having one only or both.

I answer that, As the Apostle says (Rm. 13:1), "Those things that are of God are well ordered [Vulg.: 'those that are, are ordained by God']." Now the order of things consists in this, that things are led to God by other things, as Dionysius says (Coel. Hier. iv). And hence since grace is ordained to lead men to God, this takes place in a certain order, so that some are led to God by others.

And thus there is a twofold grace: one whereby man himself is united to God, and this is called "sanctifying grace"; the other is that whereby one man cooperates with another in leading him to God, and this gift is called "gratuitous grace," since it is bestowed on a man beyond the capability of nature, and beyond the merit of the person. But whereas it is bestowed on a man, not to justify him, but rather that he may cooperate in the justification of another, it is not called sanctifying grace. And it is of this that the Apostle says (1 Cor. 12:7): "And the manifestation of the Spirit is given to every man unto utility," i.e. of others.

Reply Obj. 1: Grace is said to make pleasing, not efficiently but formally, i.e. because thereby a man is justified, and is made worthy to be called pleasing to God, according to Col. 1:21: "He hath made us worthy to be made partakers of the lot of the saints in light."

Reply Obj. 2: Grace, inasmuch as it is gratuitously given, excludes the notion of debt. Now debt may be taken in two ways: first, as arising from merit; and this regards the person whose it is to do meritorious works, according to Rm. 4:4: "Now to him that worketh, the reward is not reckoned according to grace, but according to debt." The second debt regards the condition of nature. Thus we say it is due to a man to have reason, and whatever else belongs to human nature. Yet in neither way is debt taken to mean that God is under an obligation to His creature, but rather that the creature ought to be subject to God, that the Divine ordination may be fulfilled in it, which is that a certain nature should have certain conditions or properties, and that by doing certain works it should attain to something further. And hence natural endowments are not a debt in the first sense but in the second. Hence they especially merit the name of grace.

Reply Obj. 3: Sanctifying grace adds to the notion of gratuitous grace something pertaining to the nature of grace, since it makes man pleasing to God. And hence gratuitous grace which does not do this keeps the common name, as happens in many other cases; and thus the two parts of the division are opposed as sanctifying and non-sanctifying grace.

Second Article [I–II, 112, 2]

Whether grace is fittingly divided into operating and cooperating grace?

Objection 1: It would seem that grace is not fittingly divided into operating and cooperating grace. For grace is an accident, as stated above (Question [110], Article [2]). Now no accident can act upon its subject. Therefore no grace can be called operating.

Obj. 2: Further, if grace operates anything in us it assuredly brings about justification. But not only grace works this. For Augustine says, on Jn. 14:12, "The works that I do he also shall do," says (Serm. clxix): "He Who created thee without thyself, will not justify thee without thyself." Therefore no grace ought to be called simply operating.

Obj. 3: Further, to cooperate seems to pertain to the inferior agent, and not to the principal agent. But grace works in us more than free-will, according to Rm. 9:16: "It is not of him that willeth, nor of him that runneth, but of God that sheweth mercy." Therefore no grace ought to be called cooperating.

Obj. 4: Further, division ought to rest on opposition. But to operate and to cooperate are not opposed; for one and the same thing can both operate and cooperate. Therefore grace is not fittingly divided into operating and cooperating.

On the contrary, Augustine says (De Gratia et Lib. Arbit. xvii): "God by cooperating with us, perfects what He began by operating in us, since He who perfects by cooperation with such as are willing, beings by operating that they may will." But the operations of God whereby He moves us to good pertain to grace. Therefore grace is fittingly divided into operating and cooperating.

I answer that, As stated above (Question [110], Article [2]) grace may be taken in two ways; first, as a Divine help, whereby God moves us to will and to act; secondly, as a habitual gift divinely bestowed on us.

Now in both these ways grace is fittingly divided into operating and cooperating. For the operation of an effect is not attributed to the thing moved but to the mover. Hence in that effect in which our mind is moved and does not move, but in which God is the sole mover, the operation is attributed to God, and it is with reference to this that we speak of "operating grace." But in that effect in which our mind both moves and is moved, the operation is not only attributed to God, but also to the soul; and it is with reference to this that we speak of "cooperating grace." Now there is a double act in us. First, there is the interior act of the will, and with regard to this act the will is a thing moved, and God is the mover; and especially when the will, which hitherto willed evil, begins to will good. And hence, inasmuch as God moves the human mind to this act, we speak of operating grace. But there is another, exterior act; and since it is commanded by the will, as was shown above (Question [17], Article [9]) the operation of this act is attributed to the will. And because God assists us in this act, both by strengthening our will interiorly so as to attain to the act, and by granting outwardly the capability of operating, it is with respect to this that we speak of cooperating grace. Hence after the aforesaid words Augustine subjoins: "He operates that we may will; and when we will, He cooperates that we may perfect." And thus if grace is taken for God's gratuitous motion whereby He moves us to meritorious good, it is fittingly divided into operating and cooperating grace.

But if grace is taken for the habitual gift, then again there is a double effect of grace, even as of every other form; the first of which is "being," and the second, "operation"; thus the work of heat is to make its subject hot, and to give heat outwardly. And thus habitual grace, inasmuch as it heals and justifies the soul, or makes it pleasing to God, is called operating grace; but inasmuch as it is the principle of meritorious works, which spring from the free-will, it is called cooperating grace.

Reply to Obj. 1: Inasmuch as grace is a certain accidental quality, it does not act upon the soul efficiently, but formally, as whiteness makes a surface white.

Reply to Obj. 2: God does not justify us without ourselves, because whilst we are being justified we consent to God's justification [justitiae] by a movement of our free-will. Nevertheless this movement is not the cause of grace, but the effect; hence the whole operation pertains to grace.

Reply to Obj. 3: One thing is said to cooperate with another not merely when it is a secondary agent under a principal agent, but when it helps to the end intended. Now man is helped by God to will the good, through the means of operating grace. And hence, the end being already intended, grace cooperates with us.

Reply to Obj. 4: Operating and cooperating grace are the same grace; but are distinguished by their different effects, as is plain from what has been said.

Question 112

Of the Cause of Grace
(In Five Articles)

We must now consider the cause of grace; and under this head there are five points of inquiry[of which only one is considered here]:

(1) Whether God alone is the efficient cause of grace?

First Article [I–II, Q. 112, Art. 1]

Whether God Alone Is the Cause of Grace?

Objection 1: It would seem that God alone is not the cause of grace. For it is written (John 1:17): "Grace and truth came by Jesus Christ." Now, by the name of Jesus Christ is understood not merely the Divine Nature assuming, but the created nature assumed. Therefore a creature may be the cause of grace.

Obj. 2: Further, there is this difference between the sacraments of the New Law and those of the Old, that the sacraments of the New Law cause grace, whereas the sacraments of the Old Law merely signify it. Now the sacraments of the New Law are certain visible elements. Therefore God is not the only cause of grace.

Obj. 3: Further, according to Dionysius (Coel. Hier. iii, iv, vii, viii), "Angels cleanse, enlighten, and perfect both lesser angels and men." Now the rational creature is cleansed, enlightened, and perfected by grace. Therefore God is not the only cause of grace.

On the contrary, It is written (Ps. 83:12): "The Lord will give grace and glory."

I answer that, Nothing can act beyond its species, since the cause must always be more powerful than its effect. Now the gift of grace surpasses every capability of created nature, since it is nothing short of a partaking of the Divine Nature, which exceeds every other nature. And thus it is impossible that any creature should cause grace. For it is as necessary that God alone should deify, bestowing a partaking of the Divine Nature by a participated likeness, as it is impossible that anything save fire should enkindle.

Reply Obj. 1: Christ's humanity is an "organ of His Godhead," as Damascene says (De Fide Orth. iii, 19). Now an instrument does not bring forth the action of the principal agent by its own power, but in virtue of the principal agent. Hence Christ's humanity does not cause grace by its own power, but by virtue of the Divine Nature joined to it, whereby the actions of Christ's humanity are saving actions.

Reply Obj. 2: As in the person of Christ the humanity causes our salvation by grace, the Divine power being the principal agent, so likewise in the sacraments of the New Law, which are derived from Christ, grace is instrumentally caused by the sacraments, and principally by the power of the Holy Ghost working in the sacraments, according to John 3:5: "Unless a man be born again of water and the Holy Ghost he cannot enter into the kingdom of God."

Reply Obj. 3: Angels cleanse, enlighten, and perfect angels or men, by instruction, and not by justifying them through grace. Hence Dionysius says (Coel. Hier. vii) that "this cleansing and enlightenment and perfecting is nothing else than the assumption of Divine knowledge."

Question 113

Of the Effects of Grace
(In Ten Articles)

We have now to consider the effect of grace; (1) the justification of the ungodly, which is the effect of operating grace; and (2) merit, which is the effect of cooperating grace. Under the first head there are ten points of inquiry [of which only two are considered here]:

(1) What is the justification of the ungodly?
(2) Whether grace is required for it?

First Article [I–II, Q. 113, Art. 1]

Whether the Justification of the Ungodly Is the Remission of Sins?

Objection 1: It would seem that the justification of the ungodly is not the remission of sins. For sin is opposed not

only to justice, but to all the other virtues, as stated above
(Q. 71, A. 1). Now justification signifies a certain movement
towards justice. Therefore not even remission of sin is justification, since movement is from one contrary to the other.

Obj. 2: Further, everything ought to be named from what
is predominant in it, according to *De Anima* ii, text. 49. Now
the remission of sins is brought about chiefly by faith, according to Acts 15:9: "Purifying their hearts by faith"; and by
charity, according to Prov. 10:12: "Charity covereth all sins."
Therefore the remission of sins ought to be named after faith
or charity rather than justice.

Obj. 3: Further, the remission of sins seems to be the same
as being called, for whoever is called is afar off, and we are
afar off from God by sin. But one is called before being justified according to Rom. 8:30: "And whom He called, them
He also justified." Therefore justification is not the remission
of sins.

On the contrary, On Rom. 8:30, "Whom He called, them
He also justified," the gloss says i.e. "by the remission of sins."
Therefore the remission of sins is justification.

I answer that, Justification taken passively implies a movement towards justice, as heating implies a movement towards
heat. But since justice, by its nature, implies a certain rectitude
of order, it may be taken in two ways: first, inasmuch as it
implies a right order in man's act, and thus justice is placed
amongst the virtues—either as particular justice, which directs
a man's acts by regulating them in relation to his fellowman—
or as legal justice, which directs a man's acts by regulating
them in their relation to the common good of society, as
appears from *Ethic.* v, 1.

Secondly, justice is so-called inasmuch as it implies a certain
rectitude of order in the interior disposition of a man, in so
far as what is highest in man is subject to God, and the inferior
powers of the soul are subject to the superior, i.e. to the reason;
and this disposition the Philosopher calls "justice metaphorically speaking" (Ethic. v, 11). Now this justice may be in man

in two ways: first, by simple generation, which is from priva-
tion to form; and thus justification may belong even to such
as are not in sin, when they receive this justice from God, as
Adam is said to have received original justice. Secondly, this
justice may be brought about in man by a movement from
one contrary to the other, and thus justification implies a
transmutation from the state of injustice to the aforesaid state
of justice. And it is thus we are now speaking of the justification of the ungodly, according to the Apostle (Rom. 4:5): "But
to him that worketh not, yet believeth in Him that justifieth
the ungodly," etc. And because movement is named after its
term *whereto* rather than from its term *whence,* the transmutation whereby anyone is changed by the remission of sins
from the state of ungodliness to the state of justice, borrows
its name from its term *whereto,* and is called "justification of
the ungodly."

Reply Obj. 1: Every sin, inasmuch as it implies the disorder
of a mind not subject to God, may be called injustice, as being
contrary to the aforesaid justice, according to 1 John 3:4:
"Whosoever committeth sin, committeth also iniquity; and
sin is iniquity." And thus the removal of any sin is called the
justification of the ungodly.

Reply Obj. 2: Faith and charity imply a special directing
of the human mind to God by the intellect and will; whereas
justice implies a general rectitude of order. Hence this transmutation is named after justice rather than after charity or
faith.

Reply Obj. 3: Being called refers to God's help moving and
exciting our mind to give up sin, and this motion of God is
not the remission of sins, but its cause.

Second Article [I–II, Q. 113, Art. 2]

Whether the Infusion of Grace Is Required for the Remission
of Guilt, i.e., for the Justification of the Ungodly?

Objection 1: It would seem that for the remission of guilt, which is the justification of the ungodly, no infusion of grace is required. For anyone may be moved from one contrary without being led to the other, if the contraries are not immediate. Now the state of guilt and the state of grace are not immediate contraries; for there is the middle state of innocence wherein a man has neither grace nor guilt. Hence a man may be pardoned his guilt without his being brought to a state of grace.

Obj. 2: Further, the remission of guilt consists in the Divine imputation, according to Ps. 31:2: "Blessed is the man to whom the Lord hath not imputed sin." Now the infusion of grace puts something into our soul, as stated above (Q. 110, A. 1). Hence the infusion of grace is not required for the remission of guilt.

Obj. 3: Further, no one can be subject to two contraries at once. Now some sins are contraries, as wastefulness and miserliness. Hence whoever is subject to the sin of wastefulness is not simultaneously subject to the sin of miserliness, yet it may happen that he has been subject to it hitherto. Hence by sinning with the vice of wastefulness he is freed from the sin of miserliness. And thus a sin is remitted without grace.

On the contrary, It is written (Rom. 3:24): "Justified freely by His grace."

I answer that, by sinning a man offends God as stated above (Q. 71, A. 5). Now an offense is remitted to anyone, only when the soul of the offender is at peace with the offended. Hence sin is remitted to us, when God is at peace with us, and this peace consists in the love whereby God loves us. Now God's love, considered on the part of the Divine act, is eternal and unchangeable; whereas, as regards the effect it imprints on us, it is sometimes interrupted, inasmuch as we sometimes fall short of it and once more require it. Now the effect of the Divine love in us, which is taken away by sin, is grace, whereby a man is made worthy of eternal life, from which sin shuts him out. Hence we could not conceive the remission of guilt, without the infusion of grace.

Reply Obj. 1: More is required for an offender to pardon an offense, than for one who has committed no offense, not to be hated. For it may happen amongst men that one man neither hates nor loves another. But if the other offends him, then the forgiveness of the offense can only spring from a special goodwill. Now God's goodwill is said to be restored to man by the gift of grace; and hence although a man before sinning may be without grace and without guilt, yet that he is without guilt after sinning can only be because he has grace.

Reply Obj. 2: As God's love consists not merely in the act of the Divine will but also implies a certain effect of grace, as stated above (Q. 110, A. 1), so likewise, when God does not impute sin to a man, there is implied a certain effect in him to whom the sin is not imputed; for it proceeds from the Divine love, that sin is not imputed to a man by God.

Reply Obj. 3: As Augustine says (De Nup. et Concup. i, 26), if to leave off sinning was the same as to have no sin, it would be enough if Scripture warned us thus: "'My son, hast thou sinned? do so no more?' Now this is not enough, but it is added: 'But for thy former sins also pray that they may be forgiven thee.'" For the act of sin passes, but the guilt remains, as stated above (Q. 87, A. 6). Hence when anyone passes from the sin of one vice to the sin of a contrary vice, he ceases to have the act of the former sin, but he does not cease to have the guilt, hence he may have the guilt of both sins at once. For sins are not contrary to each other on the part of their turning from God, wherein sin has its guilt.

Question 114

Of Merit (Ten Articles)

We must now consider merit, which is the effect of cooperating grace; and under this head there are ten points of inquiry [of which only two are considered here]:

(1) Whether a man can merit anything from God?
(2) Whether without grace anyone can merit eternal
life?

First Article [I–II, 114, 1]

Whether a man may merit anything from God?

Objection 1: It would seem that a man can merit nothing
from God. For no one, it would seem, merits by giving another
his due. But by all the good we do, we cannot make sufficient
return to God, since yet more is His due, as also the Philosopher says (Ethic. viii, 14). Hence it is written (Lk. 17:10):
"When you have done all these things that are commanded
you, say: We are unprofitable servants; we have done that
which we ought to do." Therefore a man can merit nothing
from God.

Obj. 2: Further, it would seem that a man merits nothing
from God, by what profits himself only, and profits God
nothing. Now by acting well, a man profits himself or another
man, but not God, for it is written (Job 35:7): "If thou do
justly, what shalt thou give Him, or what shall He receive of
thy hand." Hence a man can merit nothing from God.

Obj. 3: Further, whoever merits anything from another
makes him his debtor; for a man's wage is a debt due to him.
Now God is no one's debtor; hence it is written (Rom. 11:35):
"Who hath first given to Him, and recompense shall be made
to him?" Hence no one can merit anything from God.

On the contrary, It is written (Jer. 31:16): "There is a reward for thy work." Now a reward means something bestowed by reason of merit. Hence it would seem that a man
may merit from God.

I answer that, Merit and reward refer to the same, for a
reward means something given anyone in return for work or
toil, as a price for it. Hence, as it is an act of justice to give a
just price for anything received from another, so also is it an

act of justice to make a return for work or toil. Now justice is a kind of equality, as is clear from the Philosopher (Ethic. v, 3), and hence justice is simply between those that are simply equal; but where there is no absolute equality between them, neither is there absolute justice, but there may be a certain manner of justice, as when we speak of a father's or a master's right (Ethic. v, 6), as the Philosopher says. And hence where there is justice simply, there is the character of merit and reward simply. But where there is no simple right, but only relative, there is no character of merit simply, but only relatively, in so far as the character of justice is found there, since the child merits something from his father and the slave from his lord.

Now it is clear that between God and man there is the greatest inequality: for they are infinitely apart, and all man's good is from God. Hence there can be no justice of absolute equality between man and God, but only of a certain proportion, inasmuch as both operate after their own manner. Now the manner and measure of human virtue is in man from God. Hence man's merit with God only exists on the presupposition of the Divine ordination, so that man obtains from God, as a reward of his operation, what God gave him the power of operation for, even as natural things by their proper movements and operations obtain that to which they were ordained by God; differently, indeed, since the rational creature moves itself to act by its free-will, hence its action has the character of merit, which is not so in other creatures.

Reply to Obj. 1: Man merits, inasmuch as he does what he ought, by his free-will; otherwise the act of justice whereby anyone discharges a debt would not be meritorious.

Reply to Obj. 2: God seeks from our goods not profit, but glory, i.e. the manifestation of His goodness; even as He seeks it also in His own works. Now nothing accrues to Him, but only to ourselves, by our worship of Him. Hence we merit from God, not that by our works anything accrues to Him, but inasmuch as we work for His glory.

Reply to Obj. 3: Since our action has the character of merit, only on the presupposition of the Divine ordination, it does not follow that God is made our debtor simply, but His own, inasmuch as it is right that His will should be carried out.

Second Article [I–II, 114, 2]

Whether anyone without grace can merit eternal life?

Objection 1: It would seem that without grace anyone can merit eternal life. For man merits from God what he is divinely ordained to, as stated above (A[1]). Now man by his nature is ordained to beatitude as his end; hence, too, he naturally wishes to be blessed. Hence man by his natural endowments and without grace can merit beatitude which is eternal life.

Obj. 2: Further, the less a work is due, the more meritorious it is. Now, less due is that work which is done by one who has received fewer benefits. Hence, since he who has only natural endowments has received fewer gifts from God, than he who has gratuitous gifts as well as nature, it would seem that his works are more meritorious with God. And thus if he who has grace can merit eternal life to some extent, much more may he who has no grace.

Obj. 3: Further, God's mercy and liberality infinitely surpass human mercy and liberality. Now a man may merit from another, even though he has not hitherto had his grace. Much more, therefore, would it seem that a man without grace may merit eternal life.

On the contrary, The Apostle says (Rom. 6:23): "The grace of God, life everlasting."

I answer that, Man without grace may be looked at in two states, as was said above (Q[109], A[2]): the first, a state of perfect nature, in which Adam was before his sin; the second, a state of corrupt nature, in which we are before being restored by grace. Therefore, if we speak of man in the first state, there is only one reason why man cannot merit eternal life without grace, by his purely natural endowments, viz. because man's merit depends on the Divine pre-ordination. Now no act of anything whatsoever is divinely ordained to anything exceeding the proportion of the powers which are the principles of its act; for it is a law of Divine providence that nothing shall act beyond its powers. Now everlasting life is a good exceeding the proportion of created nature; since it exceeds its knowledge and desire, according to 1 Cor. 2:9: "Eye hath not seen, nor ear heard, neither hath it entered into the heart of man." And hence it is that no created nature is a sufficient principle of an act meritorious of eternal life, unless there is added a supernatural gift, which we call grace. But if we speak of man as existing in sin, a second reason is added to this, viz. the impediment of sin. For since sin is an offense against God, excluding us from eternal life, as is clear from what has been said above (Q[71], A[6]; Q[113], A[2]), no one existing in a state of mortal sin can merit eternal life unless first he be reconciled to God, through his sin being forgiven, which is brought about by grace. For the sinner deserves not life, but death, according to Rom. 6:23: "The wages of sin is death."

Reply to Obj. 1: God ordained human nature to attain the end of eternal life, not by its own strength, but by the help of grace; and in this way its act can be meritorious of eternal life.

Reply to Obj. 2: Without grace a man cannot have a work equal to a work proceeding from grace, since the more perfect the principle, the more perfect the action. But the objection would hold good, if we supposed the operations equal in both cases.

Reply to Obj. 3: With regard to the first reason adduced, the case is different in God and in man. For a man receives all his power of well-doing from God, and not from man. Hence a man can merit nothing from God except by His gift, which the Apostle expresses aptly saying (Rom. 11:35): "Who hath first given to Him, and recompense shall be made to him?" But man may merit from man, before he has received anything from him, by what he has received from God.

But as regards the second proof taken from the impediment of sin, the case is similar with man and God, since one man cannot merit from another whom he has offended, unless he makes satisfaction to him and is reconciled.

On the Virtues [Questions 55, 62 and 63]

Question 55.

Of the Virtues, as to their Essence
(In Four Articles)

We come now to the consideration of habits specifically. And since habits, as we have said (Q. 54, A. 3), are divided into good and bad, we must speak in the first place of good habits, which are virtues, and of other matters connected with them, namely the Gifts, Beatitudes and Fruits; in the second place, of bad habits, namely of vices and sins. Now five things must be considered about virtues: (1) the essence of virtue; (2) its subject; (3) the division of virtue; (4) the cause of virtue; (5) certain properties of virtue.

Under the first head, there are four points of inquiry:

(1) Whether human virtue is a habit?
(2) Whether it is an operative habit?
(3) Whether it is a good habit?
(4) Of the definition of virtue.

First Article [I–II, Q. 55, Art. 1]

Whether Human Virtue Is a Habit?

Objection 1: It would seem that human virtue is not a habit: For virtue is "the limit of power" (De Coelo i, text. 116). But the limit of anything is reducible to the genus of that of which it is the limit; as a point is reducible to the genus of line. Therefore virtue is reducible to the genus of power, and not to the genus of habit.

Obj. 2: Further, Augustine says (De Lib. Arb. ii) [*Retract. ix; cf. De Lib. Arb. ii, 19] that "virtue is good use of free-will." But use of free-will is an act. Therefore virtue is not a habit, but an act.

Obj. 3: Further, we do not merit by our habits, but by our actions: otherwise a man would merit continually, even while asleep. But we do merit by our virtues. Therefore virtues are not habits, but acts.

Obj. 4: Further, Augustine says (De Moribus Eccl. xv) that "virtue is the order of love," and (QQ. lxxxiii, qu. 30) that "the ordering which is called virtue consists in enjoying what we ought to enjoy, and using what we ought to use." Now order, or ordering, denominates either an action or a relation. Therefore virtue is not a habit, but an action or a relation.

Obj. 5: Further, just as there are human virtues, so are there natural virtues. But natural virtues are not habits, but powers. Neither therefore are human virtues habits.

On the contrary, The Philosopher says (Categor. vi) that science and virtue are habits.

I answer that, Virtue denotes a certain perfection of a power. Now a thing's perfection is considered chiefly in regard to its end. But the end of power is act. Wherefore power is said to be perfect, according as it is determinate to its act.

Now there are some powers which of themselves are determinate to their acts; for instance, the active natural powers. And therefore these natural powers are in themselves called virtues. But the rational powers, which are proper to man, are not determinate to one particular action, but are inclined indifferently to many: and they are determinate to acts by means of habits, as is clear from what we have said above (Q. 49, A. 4). Therefore human virtues are habits.

Reply Obj. 1: Sometimes we give the name of a virtue to that to which the virtue is directed, namely, either to its object, or to its act: for instance, we give the name Faith, to that which we believe, or to the act of believing, as also to the habit by which we believe. When therefore we say that "virtue is the limit of power," virtue is taken for the object of virtue. For the furthest point to which a power can reach, is said to be its virtue; for instance, if a man can carry a hundredweight and not more, his virtue [*In English we should say 'strength,' which is the original signification of the Latin 'virtus': thus we speak of an engine being so many horsepower, to indicate its 'strength'] is put at a hundredweight, and not at sixty. But the objection takes virtue as being essentially the limit of power.

Reply Obj. 2: Good use of free-will is said to be a virtue, in the same sense as above (ad 1); that is to say, because it is that to which virtue is directed as to its proper act. For the act of virtue is nothing else than the good use of free-will.

Reply Obj. 3: We are said to merit by something in two ways. First, as by merit itself, just as we are said to run by running; and thus we merit by acts. Secondly, we are said to merit by something as by the principle whereby we merit, as we are said to run by the motive power; and thus are we said to merit by virtues and habits.

Reply Obj. 4: When we say that virtue is the order or ordering of love, we refer to the end to which virtue is ordered: because in us love is set in order by virtue.

Reply Obj. 5: Natural powers are of themselves determinate to one act: not so the rational powers. And so there is no comparison, as we have said.

Second Article [I–II, Q. 55, Art. 2]

Whether Human Virtue Is an Operative Habit?

Objection 1: It would seem that it is not essential to human virtue to be an operative habit. For Tully says (Tuscul. iv) that as health and beauty belong to the body, so virtue belongs to the soul. But health and beauty are not operative habits. Therefore neither is virtue.

Obj. 2: Further, in natural things we find virtue not only in reference to act, but also in reference to being: as is clear from the Philosopher (De Coelo i), since some have a virtue to be always, while some have a virtue to be not always, but at some definite time. Now as natural virtue is in natural things, so is human virtue in rational beings. Therefore also human virtue is referred not only to act, but also to being.

Obj. 3: Further, the Philosopher says (Phys. vii, text. 17) that virtue "is the disposition of a perfect thing to that which is best." Now the best thing to which man needs to be disposed by virtue is God Himself, as Augustine proves (De Moribus Eccl. 3, 6, 14) to Whom the soul is disposed by being made like to Him. Therefore it seems that virtue is a quality of the soul in reference to God, likening it, as it were, to Him; and not in reference to operation. It is not, therefore, an operative habit.

On the contrary, The Philosopher (Ethic. ii, 6) says that "virtue of a thing is that which makes its work good."

I answer that, Virtue, from the very nature of the word, implies some perfection of power, as we have said above (A. 1). Wherefore, since power [*The one Latin word *potentia*is rendered 'potentiality' in the first case, and 'power' in the second] is of two kinds, namely, power in reference to being, and power in reference to act; the perfection of each of these is called virtue. But power in reference to being is on the part of matter, which is potential being, whereas power in reference to act, is on the part of the form, which is the principle of action, since everything acts in so far as it is in act.

Now man is so constituted that the body holds the place of matter, the soul that of form. The body, indeed, man has in common with other animals; and the same is to be said of the forces which are common to the soul and body: and only those forces which are proper to the soul, namely, the rational forces, belong to man alone. And therefore, human virtue, of which we are speaking now, cannot belong to the body, but belongs only to that which is proper to the soul. Wherefore human virtue does not imply reference to being, but rather to act. Consequently it is essential to human virtue to be an operative habit.

Reply Obj. 1: Mode of action follows on the disposition of the agent: for such as a thing is, such is its act. And therefore, since virtue is the principle of some kind of operation, there must needs pre-exist in the operator in respect of virtue some corresponding disposition. Now virtue causes an ordered operation. Therefore virtue itself is an ordered disposition of the soul, in so far as, to wit, the powers of the soul are in some way ordered to one another, and to that which is outside. Hence virtue, inasmuch as it is a suitable disposition of the soul, is like health and beauty, which are suitable dispositions of the body. But this does not hinder virtue from being a principle of operation.

Reply Obj. 2: Virtue which is referred to being is not proper to man; but only that virtue which is referred to works of reason, which are proper to man.

Reply Obj. 3: As God's substance is His act, the highest likeness of man to God is in respect of some operation. Wherefore, as we have said above (Q. 3, A. 2), happiness or bliss by which man is made most perfectly conformed to God, and which is the end of human life, consists in an operation.

Third Article [I–II, Q. 55, Art. 3]

Whether Human Virtue Is a Good Habit?

Objection 1: It would seem that it is not essential to virtue that it should be a good habit. For sin is always taken in a bad sense. But there is a virtue even of sin; according to 1 Cor. 15:56: "The virtue [Douay: 'strength'] of sin is the Law." Therefore virtue is not always a good habit.

Obj. 2: Further, Virtue corresponds to power. But power is not only referred to good, but also to evil: according to Isa. 5: "Woe to you that are mighty to drink wine, and stout men at drunkenness." Therefore virtue also is referred to good and evil.

Obj. 3: Further, according to the Apostle (2 Cor. 12:9): "Virtue [Douay: 'power'] is made perfect in infirmity." But infirmity is an evil. Therefore virtue is referred not only to good, but also to evil.

On the contrary, Augustine says (De Moribus Eccl. vi): "No one can doubt that virtue makes the soul exceeding good": and the Philosopher says (Ethic. ii, 6): "Virtue is that which makes its possessor good, and his work good likewise."

I answer that, As we have said above (A. 1), virtue implies a perfection of power: wherefore the virtue of a thing is fixed by the limit of its power (De Coelo i). Now the limit of any power must needs be good: for all evil implies defect; wherefore Dionysius says (Div. Hom. ii) that every evil is a weakness. And for this reason the virtue of a thing must be regarded in reference to good. Therefore human virtue which is an operative habit, is a good habit, productive of good works.

Reply Obj. 1: Just as bad things are said metaphorically to be perfect, so are they said to be good: for we speak of a perfect thief or robber; and of a good thief or robber, as the Philosopher explains (Metaph. v, text. 21). In this way therefore virtue is applied to evil things: so that the "virtue" of sin is said to be law, in so far as occasionally sin is aggravated through the law, so as to attain to the limit of its possibility.

Reply Obj. 2: The evil of drunkenness and excessive drink, consists in a falling away from the order of reason. Now it happens that, together with this falling away from reason, some lower power is perfect in reference to that which belongs to its own kind, even in direct opposition to reason, or with some falling away therefrom. But the perfection of that power, since it is compatible with a falling away from reason, cannot be called a human virtue.

Reply Obj. 3: Reason is shown to be so much the more perfect, according as it is able to overcome or endure more easily the weakness of the body and of the lower powers. And therefore human virtue, which is attributed to reason, is said to be "made perfect in infirmity," not of the reason indeed, but of the body and of the lower powers.

Fourth Article [I–II, Q. 55, Art. 4]

Whether Virtue Is Suitably Defined?

Objection 1: It would seem that the definition, usually given, of virtue, is not suitable, to wit: "Virtue is a good quality of the mind, by which we live righteously, of which no one can make bad use, which God works in us, without us." For virtue is man's goodness, since virtue it is that makes its subject good. But goodness does not seem to be good, as neither is whiteness white. It is therefore unsuitable to describe virtue as a "good quality."

Obj. 2: Further, no difference is more common than its genus; since it is that which divides the genus. But good is more common than quality, since it is convertible with being. Therefore "good" should not be put in the definition of virtue, as a difference of quality.

Obj. 3: Further, as Augustine says (De Trin. xii, 3): "When we come across anything that is not common to us and the beasts of the field, it is something appertaining to the mind." But there are virtues even of the irrational parts; as the Philosopher says (Ethic. iii, 10). Every virtue, therefore, is not a good quality "of the mind."

Obj. 4: Further, righteousness seems to belong to justice; whence the righteous are called just. But justice is a species of virtue. It is therefore unsuitable to put "righteous" in the definition of virtue, when we say that virtue is that "by which we live righteously."

Obj. 5: Further, whoever is proud of a thing, makes bad use of it. But many are proud of virtue, for Augustine says in his Rule, that "pride lies in wait for good works in order to slay them." It is untrue, therefore, "that no one can make bad use of virtue."

Obj. 6: Further, man is justified by virtue. But Augustine commenting on John 15:11: "He shall do greater things than these," says [*Tract. xxvii in Joan.: Serm. xv de Verb. Ap. 11]: "He who created thee without thee, will not justify thee without thee." It is therefore unsuitable to say that "God works virtue in us, without us."

On the contrary, We have the authority of Augustine from whose words this definition is gathered, and principally in *De Libero Arbitrio* ii, 19.

I answer that, This definition comprises perfectly the whole essential notion of virtue. For the perfect essential notion of anything is gathered from all its causes. Now the above definition comprises all the causes of virtue. For the formal cause of virtue, as of everything, is gathered from its genus and difference, when it is defined as "a good quality": for "quality" is the genus of virtue, and the difference, "good." But the definition would be more suitable if for "quality" we substitute "habit," which is the proximate genus.

Now virtue has no matter "out of which" it is formed, as neither has any other accident; but it has matter "about which" it is concerned, and matter "in which" it exists, namely, the subject. The matter about which virtue is concerned is its object, and this could not be included in the above definition, because the object fixes the virtue to a certain species, and here we are giving the definition of virtue in general. And so for material cause we have the subject, which is mentioned when we say that virtue is a good quality "of the mind."

The end of virtue, since it is an operative habit, is operation. But it must be observed that some operative habits are always referred to evil, as vicious habits: others are sometimes referred to good, sometimes to evil; for instance, opinion is referred both to the true and to the untrue: whereas virtue is a habit which is always referred to good: and so the distinction of virtue from those habits which are always referred to evil, is expressed in the words "by which we live righteously": and its distinction from those habits which are sometimes directed unto good, sometimes unto evil, in the words, "of which no one makes bad use."

Lastly, God is the efficient cause of infused virtue, to which this definition applies; and this is expressed in the words "which God works in us without us." If we omit this phrase, the remainder of the definition will apply to all virtues in general, whether acquired or infused.

Reply Obj. 1: That which is first seized by the intellect is being: wherefore everything that we apprehend we consider as being, and consequently as one, and as good, which are convertible with being. Wherefore we say that essence is being and is one and is good; and that oneness is being and one and good: and in like manner goodness. But this is not the case with specific forms, as whiteness and health; for everything that we apprehend, is not apprehended with the notion of white and healthy. We must, however, observe that, as accidents and non-subsistent forms are called beings, not as if they themselves had being, but because things are by them; so also are they called good or one, not by some distinct goodness or oneness, but because by them something is good or one. So also is virtue called good, because by it something is good.

Reply Obj. 2: Good, which is put in the definition of virtue, is not good in general which is convertible with being, and which extends further than quality, but the good as fixed by reason, with regard to which Dionysius says (Div. Nom. iv) "that the good of the soul is to be in accord with reason."

Reply Obj. 3: Virtue cannot be in the irrational part of the soul, except in so far as this participates in the reason (Ethic. i, 13). And therefore reason, or the mind, is the proper subject of virtue.

Reply Obj. 4: Justice has a righteousness of its own by which it puts those outward things right which come into human use, and are the proper matter of justice, as we shall show further on (Q. 60, A. 2; II-II, Q. 58, A. 8). But the righteousness which denotes order to a due end and to the Divine law, which is the rule of the human will, as stated above (Q. 19, A. 4), is common to all virtues.

Reply Obj. 5: One can make bad use of a virtue objectively, for instance by having evil thoughts about a virtue, e.g. by hating it, or by being proud of it: but one cannot make bad use of virtue as principle of action, so that an act of virtue be evil.

Reply Obj. 6: Infused virtue is caused in us by God without any action on our part, but not without our consent. This is the sense of the words, "which God works in us without us." As to those things which are done by us, God causes them in us, yet not without action on our part, for He works in every will and in every nature.

Question 62

Of the Theological Virtues
(In Four Articles)

We must now consider the Theological Virtues: under which head there are four points of inquiry:

(1) Whether there are any theological virtues?
(2) Whether the theological virtues are distinct from the intellectual and moral virtues?

(3) How many, and which are they?
(4) Of their order.

First Article [I–II, Q. 62, Art. 1]

Whether There Are Any Theological Virtues?

Objection 1: It would seem that there are not any theological virtues. For according to *Phys.* vii, text. 17, "Virtue is the disposition of a perfect thing to that which is best: and by perfect, I mean that which is disposed according to nature." But that which is Divine is above man's nature. Therefore the theological virtues are not virtues of a man.

Obj. 2: Further, theological virtues are quasi-Divine virtues. But the Divine virtues are exemplars, as stated above (Q. 61, A. 5), which are not in us but in God. Therefore the theological virtues are not virtues of man.

Obj. 3: Further, the theological virtues are so called because they direct us to God, Who is the first beginning and last end of all things. But by the very nature of his reason and will, man is directed to his first beginning and last end. Therefore there is no need for any habits of theological virtue, to direct the reason and will to God.

On the contrary, The precepts of the Law are about acts of virtue. Now the Divine Law contains precepts about the acts of faith, hope, and charity: for it is written (Ecclus. 2:8, seqq.): "Ye that fear the Lord believe Him," and again, "hope in Him," and again, "love Him." Therefore faith, hope, and charity are virtues directing us to God. Therefore they are theological virtues.

I answer that, Man is perfected by virtue, for those actions whereby he is directed to happiness, as was explained above (Q. 5, A. 7). Now man's happiness is twofold, as was also stated above (Q. 5, A. 5). One is proportionate to human nature, a happiness, to wit, which man can obtain by means of his natural principles. The other is a happiness surpassing man's nature, and which man can obtain by the power of God alone, by a kind of participation of the Godhead, about which it is written (2 Pet. 1:4) that by Christ we are made "partakers of the Divine nature." And because such happiness surpasses the capacity of human nature, man's natural principles which enable him to act well according to his capacity, do not suffice to direct man to this same happiness. Hence it is necessary for man to receive from God some additional principles, whereby he may be directed to supernatural happiness, even as he is directed to his connatural end, by means of his natural principles, albeit not without Divine assistance. Such like principles are called "theological virtues": first, because their object is God, inasmuch as they direct us aright to God: secondly, because they are infused in us by God alone: thirdly, because these virtues are not made known to us, save by Divine revelation, contained in Holy Writ.

Reply Obj. 1: A certain nature may be ascribed to a certain thing in two ways. First, essentially: and thus these theological virtues surpass the nature of man. Secondly, by participation, as kindled wood partakes of the nature of fire: and thus, after a fashion, man becomes a partaker of the Divine Nature, as stated above: so that these virtues are proportionate to man in respect of the Nature of which he is made a partaker.

Reply Obj. 2: These virtues are called Divine, not as though God were virtuous by reason of them, but because of them God makes us virtuous, and directs us to Himself. Hence they are not exemplar but exemplate virtues.

Reply Obj. 3: The reason and will are naturally directed to God, inasmuch as He is the beginning and end of nature, but in proportion to nature. But the reason and will, according to their nature, are not sufficiently directed to Him in so far as He is the object of supernatural happiness.

Second Article [I–II, Q. 62, Art. 2]

Whether the Theological Virtues Are Distinct from the Intellectual and Moral Virtues?

Objection 1: It would seem that the theological virtues are not distinct from the moral and intellectual virtues. For the theological virtues, if they be in a human soul, must needs perfect it, either as to the intellective, or as to the appetitive part. Now the virtues which perfect the intellective part are called intellectual; and the virtues which perfect the appetitive part, are called moral. Therefore, the theological virtues are not distinct from the moral and intellectual virtues.

Obj. 2: Further, the theological virtues are those which direct us to God. Now, among the intellectual virtues there is one which directs us to God: this is wisdom, which is about Divine things, since it considers the highest cause. Therefore the theological virtues are not distinct from the intellectual virtues.

Obj. 3: Further, Augustine (De Moribus Eccl. xv) shows how the four cardinal virtues are the "order of love." Now love is charity, which is a theological virtue. Therefore the moral virtues are not distinct from the theological.

On the contrary, That which is above man's nature is distinct from that which is according to his nature. But the theological virtues are above man's nature; while the intellectual and moral virtues are in proportion to his nature, as clearly shown above (Q. 58, A. 3). Therefore they are distinct from one another.

I answer that, As stated above (Q. 54, A. 2, ad 1), habits are specifically distinct from one another in respect of the formal difference of their objects. Now the object of the theological virtues is God Himself, Who is the last end of all, as surpassing the knowledge of our reason. On the other hand, the object of the intellectual and moral virtues is something comprehensible to human reason. Wherefore the theological virtues are specifically distinct from the moral and intellectual virtues.

Reply Obj. 1: The intellectual and moral virtues perfect man's intellect and appetite according to the capacity of human nature; the theological virtues, supernaturally.

Reply Obj. 2: The wisdom which the Philosopher (Ethic. vi, 3, 7) reckons as an intellectual virtue, considers Divine things so far as they are open to the research of human reason. Theological virtue, on the other hand, is about those same things so far as they surpass human reason.

Reply Obj. 3: Though charity is love, yet love is not always charity. When, then, it is stated that every virtue is the order of love, this can be understood either of love in the general sense, or of the love of charity. If it be understood of love, commonly so called, then each virtue is stated to be the order of love, in so far as each cardinal virtue requires ordinate emotions; and love is the root and cause of every emotion, as stated above (Q. 27, A. 4; Q. 28, A. 6, ad 2; Q. 41, A. 2, ad 1). If, however, it be understood of the love of charity, it does not mean that every other virtue is charity essentially: but that all other virtues depend on charity in some way, as we shall show further on (Q. 65, AA. 2, 5; II–II, Q. 23, A. 7).

Third Article [I–II, Q. 62, Art. 3]

Whether Faith, Hope, and Charity Are Fittingly Reckoned as Theological Virtues?

Objection 1: It would seem that faith, hope, and charity are not fittingly reckoned as three theological virtues. For the theological virtues are in relation to Divine happiness, what the natural inclination is in relation to the connatural end. Now among the virtues directed to the connatural end there is but one natural virtue, viz. the understanding of principles. Therefore there should be but one theological virtue.

Obj. 2: Further, the theological virtues are more perfect than the intellectual and moral virtues. Now faith is not reckoned among the intellectual virtues, but is something less than a virtue, since it is imperfect knowledge. Likewise hope is not reckoned among the moral virtues, but is something less than a virtue, since it is a passion. Much less therefore should they be reckoned as theological virtues.

Obj. 3: Further, the theological virtues direct man's soul to God. Now man's soul cannot be directed to God, save through

the intellective part, wherein are the intellect and will. Therefore there should be only two theological virtues, one perfecting the intellect, the other, the will.

On the contrary, The Apostle says (1 Cor. 13:13): "Now
there remain faith, hope, charity, these three."

I answer that, As stated above (A. 1), the theological virtues
direct man to supernatural happiness in the same way as by
the natural inclination man is directed to his connatural end.
Now the latter happens in respect of two things. First, in
respect of the reason or intellect, in so far as it contains the
first universal principles which are known to us by the natural
light of the intellect, and which are reason's starting-point,
both in speculative and in practical matters. Secondly, through
the rectitude of the will which tends naturally to good as defined
by reason.

But these two fall short of the order of supernatural happiness, according to 1 Cor. 2:9: "The eye hath not seen, nor
ear heard, neither hath it entered into the heart of man, what
things God hath prepared for them that love Him." Consequently in respect of both the above things man needed to
receive in addition something supernatural to direct him to
a supernatural end. First, as regards the intellect, man receives
certain supernatural principles, which are held by means of
a Divine light: these are the articles of faith, about which is
faith. Secondly, the will is directed to this end, both as to that
end as something attainable—and this pertains to hope—and
as to a certain spiritual union, whereby the will is, so to speak,
transformed into that end—and this belongs to charity. For
the appetite of a thing is moved and tends towards its connatural end naturally; and this movement is due to a certain
conformity of the thing with its end.

Reply Obj. 1: The intellect requires intelligible species
whereby to understand: consequently there is need of a natural
habit in addition to the power. But the very nature of the will
suffices for it to be directed naturally to the end, both as to
the intention of the end and as to its conformity with the end.
But the nature of the power is insufficient in either of these

respects, for the will to be directed to things that are above its nature. Consequently there was need for an additional supernatural habit in both respects.

Reply Obj. 2: Faith and hope imply a certain imperfection: since faith is of things unseen, and hope, of things not possessed. Hence faith and hope, in things that are subject to human power, fall short of the notion of virtue. But faith and hope in things which are above the capacity of human nature surpass all virtue that is in proportion to man, according to 1 Cor. 1:25: "The weakness of God is stronger than men."

Reply Obj. 3: Two things pertain to the appetite, viz. movement to the end, and conformity with the end by means of love. Hence there must needs be two theological virtues in the human appetite, namely, hope and charity.

Fourth Article [I–II, Q. 62, Art. 4]

Whether Faith Precedes Hope, and Hope Charity?

Objection 1: It would seem that the order of the theological virtues is not that faith precedes hope, and hope charity. For the root precedes that which grows from it. Now charity is the root of all the virtues, according to Eph. 3:17: "Being rooted and founded in charity." Therefore charity precedes the others.

Obj. 2: Further, Augustine says (De Doctr. Christ. i): "A man cannot love what he does not believe to exist. But if he believes and loves, by doing good works he ends in hoping." Therefore it seems that faith precedes charity, and charity hope.

Obj. 3: Further, love is the principle of all our emotions, as stated above (A. 2, ad 3). Now hope is a kind of emotion, since it is a passion, as stated above (Q. 25, A. 2). Therefore charity, which is love, precedes hope.

On the contrary, The Apostle enumerates them thus (1 Cor. 13:13): "Now there remain faith, hope, charity."

I answer that, Order is twofold: order of generation, and order of perfection. By order of generation, in respect of which matter precedes form, and the imperfect precedes the perfect, in one same subject faith precedes hope, and hope charity, as to their acts: because habits are all infused together. For the movement of the appetite cannot tend to anything, either by hoping or loving, unless that thing be apprehended by the sense or by the intellect. Now it is by faith that the intellect apprehends the object of hope and love. Hence in the order of generation, faith precedes hope and charity. In like manner a man loves a thing because he apprehends it as his good. Now from the very fact that a man hopes to be able to obtain some good through someone, he looks on the man in whom he hopes as a good of his own. Hence for the very reason that a man hopes in someone, he proceeds to love him: so that in the order of generation, hope precedes charity as regards their respective acts.

But in the order of perfection, charity precedes faith and hope: because both faith and hope are quickened by charity, and receive from charity their full complement as virtues. For thus charity is the mother and the root of all the virtues, inasmuch as it is the form of them all, as we shall state further on (II-II, Q. 23, A. 8).

This suffices for the Reply to the First Objection.

Reply Obj. 2: Augustine is speaking of that hope whereby a man hopes to obtain bliss through the merits which he has already: this belongs to hope quickened by and following charity. But it is possible for a man before having charity, to hope through merits not already possessed, but which he hopes to possess.

Reply Obj. 3: As stated above (Q. 40, A. 7), in treating of the passions, hope regards two things. One as its principal object, viz. the good hoped for. With regard to this, love always precedes hope: for good is never hoped for unless it be desired and loved. Hope also regards the person from whom a man hopes to be able to obtain some good. With regard to this, hope precedes love at first; though afterwards hope is in-creased by love. Because from the fact that a man thinks that he can obtain a good through someone, he begins to love him: and from the fact that he loves him, he then hopes all the more in him.

Question 63

Of the Cause of Virtues
(In Four Articles)

We must now consider the cause of virtues; and under this head there are four points of inquiry:

(1) Whether virtue is in us by nature?
(2) Whether any virtue is caused in us by habituation?
(3) Whether any moral virtues are in us by infusion?
(4) Whether virtue acquired by habituation, is of the same species as infused virtue?

First Article [I–II, Q. 63, Art. 1]

Whether Virtue Is in Us by Nature?

Objection 1: It would seem that virtue is in us by nature. For Damascene says (De Fide Orth. iii, 14): "Virtues are natural to us and are equally in all of us." And Antony says in his sermon to the monks: "If the will contradicts nature it is perverse, if it follow nature it is virtuous." Moreover, a gloss on Matt. 4:23, "Jesus went about," etc., says: "He taught them natural virtues, i.e. chastity, justice, humility, which man possesses naturally."

Obj. 2: Further, the virtuous good consists in accord with reason, as was clearly shown above (Q. 55, A. 4, ad 2). But that which accords with reason is natural to man; since reason is part of man's nature. Therefore virtue is in man by nature.

Obj. 3: Further, that which is in us from birth is said to be natural to us. Now virtues are in some from birth: for it is written (Job 31:18): "From my infancy mercy grew up with me; and it came out with me from my mother's womb." Therefore virtue is in man by nature.

On the contrary, Whatever is in man by nature is common to all men, and is not taken away by sin, since even in the demons natural gifts remain, as Dionysius states (Div. Nom. iv). But virtue is not in all men; and is cast out by sin. Therefore it is not in man by nature.

I answer that, With regard to corporeal forms, it has been maintained by some that they are wholly from within, by those, for instance, who upheld the theory of "latent forms" [*Anaxagoras; Cf. I, Q. 45, A. 8; Q. 65, A. 4]. Others held that forms are entirely from without, those, for instance, who thought that corporeal forms originated from some separate cause. Others, however, esteemed that they are partly from within, in so far as they pre-exist potentially in matter; and partly from without, in so far as they are brought into act by the agent.

In like manner with regard to sciences and virtues, some held that they are wholly from within, so that all virtues and sciences would pre-exist in the soul naturally, but that the hindrances to science and virtue, which are due to the soul being weighed down by the body, are removed by study and practice, even as iron is made bright by being polished. This was the opinion of the Platonists. Others said that they are wholly from without, being due to the inflow of the active intellect, as Avicenna maintained. Others said that sciences and virtues are within us by nature, so far as we are adapted to them, but not in their perfection: this is the teaching of the Philosopher (Ethic. ii, 1), and is nearer the truth.

To make this clear, it must be observed that there are two ways in which something is said to be natural to a man; one is according to his specific nature, the other according to his individual nature. And, since each thing derives its species from its form, and its individuation from matter, and, again, since man's form is his rational soul, while his matter is his body, whatever belongs to him in respect of his rational soul, is natural to him in respect of his specific nature; while whatever belongs to him in respect of the particular temperament of his body, is natural to him in respect of his individual nature. For whatever is natural to man in respect of his body, considered as part of his species, is to be referred, in a way, to the soul, in so far as this particular body is adapted to this particular soul.

In both these ways virtue is natural to man inchoatively. This is so in respect of the specific nature, in so far as in man's reason are to be found instilled by nature certain naturally known principles of both knowledge and action, which are the nurseries of intellectual and moral virtues, and in so far as there is in the will a natural appetite for good in accordance with reason. Again, this is so in respect of the individual nature, in so far as by reason of a disposition in the body, some are disposed either well or ill to certain virtues: because, to wit, certain sensitive powers are acts of certain parts of the body, according to the disposition of which these powers are helped or hindered in the exercise of their acts, and, in consequence, the rational powers also, which the aforesaid sensitive powers assist. In this way one man has a natural aptitude for science, another for fortitude, another for temperance: and in these ways, both intellectual and moral virtues are in us by way of a natural aptitude, inchoatively, but not perfectly, since nature is determined to one, while the perfection of these virtues does not depend on one particular mode of action, but on various modes, in respect of the various matters, which constitute the sphere of virtue's action, and according to various circumstances.

It is therefore evident that all virtues are in us by nature, according to aptitude and inchoation, but not according to perfection, except the theological virtues, which are entirely from without.

This suffices for the Replies to the Objections. For the first two argue about the nurseries of virtue which are in us by nature, inasmuch as we are rational beings. The third objection must be taken in the sense that, owing to the natural disposition which the body has from birth, one has an aptitude for pity, another for living temperately, another for some other virtue.

Second Article [I–II, Q. 63, Art. 2]

Whether Any Virtue Is Caused in Us by Habituation?

Objection 1: It would seem that virtues can not be caused in us by habituation. Because a gloss of Augustine [*Cf. Lib. Sentent. Prosperi cvi.] commenting on Rom. 14:23, "All that is not of faith is sin," says: "The whole life of an unbeliever is a sin: and there is no good without the Sovereign Good. Where knowledge of the truth is lacking, virtue is a mockery even in the best behaved people." Now faith cannot be acquired by means of works, but is caused in us by God, according to Eph. 2:8: "By grace you are saved through faith." Therefore no acquired virtue can be in us by habituation.

Obj. 2: Further, sin and virtue are contraries, so that they are incompatible. Now man cannot avoid sin except by the grace of God, according to Wis. 8:21: "I knew that I could not otherwise be continent, except God gave it." Therefore neither can any virtues be caused in us by habituation, but only by the gift of God.

Obj. 3: Further, actions which lead toward virtue, lack the perfection of virtue. But an effect cannot be more perfect than its cause. Therefore a virtue cannot be caused by actions that precede it.

On the contrary, Dionysius says (Div. Nom. iv) that good is more efficacious than evil. But vicious habits are caused by evil acts. Much more, therefore, can virtuous habits be caused by good acts.

I answer that, We have spoken above (Q. 51, AA. 2, 3) in a general way about the production of habits from acts; and speaking now in a special way of this matter in relation to virtue, we must take note that, as stated above (Q. 55, AA. 3, 4), man's virtue perfects him in relation to good. Now since the notion of good consists in "mode, species, and order," as Augustine states (De Nat. Boni. iii) or in "number, weight, and measure," as expressed in Wis. 11:21, man's good must needs be appraised with respect to some rule. Now this rule is two-fold, as stated above (Q. 19, AA. 3, 4), viz. human reason and Divine Law. And since Divine Law is the higher rule, it extends to more things, so that whatever is ruled by human reason, is ruled by the Divine Law too; but the converse does not hold.

It follows that human virtue directed to the good which is defined according to the rule of human reason can be caused by human acts: inasmuch as such acts proceed from reason, by whose power and rule the aforesaid good is established. On the other hand, virtue which directs man to good as defined by the Divine Law, and not by human reason, cannot be caused by human acts, the principle of which is reason, but is produced in us by the Divine operation alone. Hence Augustine in giving the definition of the latter virtue inserts the words, "which God works in us without us" (Super Ps. 118, Serm. xxvi). It is also of these virtues that the First Objection holds good.

Reply Obj. 2: Mortal sin is incompatible with divinely infused virtue, especially if this be considered in its perfect state. But actual sin, even mortal, is compatible with humanly acquired virtue; because the use of a habit in us is subject to our will, as stated above (Q. 49, A. 3): and one sinful act does not destroy a habit of acquired virtue, since it is not an act but a habit, that is directly contrary to a habit. Wherefore, though man cannot avoid mortal sin without grace, so as never to sin mortally, yet he is not hindered from acquiring a habit of virtue, whereby he may abstain from evil in the majority of cases, and chiefly in matters most opposed to reason. There are also certain mortal sins which man can nowise avoid without grace, those, namely, which are directly opposed to the theological virtues, which are in us through the gift of grace. This, however, will be more fully explained later (Q. 109, A. 4).

Reply Obj. 3: As stated above (A. 1; Q. 51, A. 1), certain seeds or principles of acquired virtue pre-exist in us by nature. These principles are more excellent than the virtues acquired through them: thus the understanding of speculative principles is more excellent than the science of conclusions, and the natural rectitude of the reason is more excellent than the rectification of the appetite which results through the appetite partaking of reason, which rectification belongs to moral virtue. Accordingly human acts, in so far as they proceed from higher principles, can cause acquired human virtues.

Third Article [I–II, Q. 63, Art. 3]

Whether Any Moral Virtues Are in Us by Infusion?

Objection 1: It would seem that no virtues besides the theological virtues are infused in us by God. Because God does not do by Himself, save perhaps sometimes miraculously, those things that can be done by second causes; for, as Dionysius says (Coel. Hier. iv), "it is God's rule to bring about extremes through the mean." Now intellectual and moral virtues can be caused in us by our acts, as stated above (A. 2). Therefore it is not reasonable that they should be caused in us by infusion.

Obj. 2: Further, much less superfluity is found in God's works than in the works of nature. Now the theological virtues suffice to direct us to supernatural good. Therefore there are no other supernatural virtues needing to be caused in us by God.

Obj. 3: Further, nature does not employ two means where one suffices: much less does God. But God sowed the seeds of virtue in our souls, according to a gloss on Heb. 1 [*Cf. Jerome on Gal. 1: 15, 16]. Therefore it is unfitting for Him to cause in us other virtues by means of infusion.

On the contrary, It is written (Wis. 8:7): "She teacheth temperance and prudence and justice and fortitude."

I answer that, Effects must needs be proportionate to their causes and principles. Now all virtues, intellectual and moral, that are acquired by our actions, arise from certain natural principles preexisting in us, as above stated (A. 1; Q. 51, A. 1): instead of which natural principles, God bestows on us the theological virtues, whereby we are directed to a supernatural end, as stated (Q. 62, A. 1). Wherefore we need to receive from God other habits corresponding, in due proportion, to the theological virtues, which habits are to the theological virtues, what the moral and intellectual virtues are to the natural principles of virtue.

Reply Obj. 1: Some moral and intellectual virtues can indeed be caused in us by our actions: but such are not proportionate to the theological virtues. Therefore it was necessary for us to receive, from God immediately, others that are proportionate to these virtues.

Reply Obj. 2: The theological virtues direct us sufficiently to our supernatural end, inchoatively: i.e. to God Himself immediately. But the soul needs further to be perfected by infused virtues in regard to other things, yet in relation to God.

Reply Obj. 3: The power of those naturally instilled principles does not extend beyond the capacity of nature. Consequently man needs in addition to be perfected by other principles in relation to his supernatural end.

Fourth Article [I–II, Q. 63, Art. 4]

Whether Virtue by Habituation Belongs to the Same Species as Infused Virtue?

Objection 1: It would seem that infused virtue does not differ in species from acquired virtue. Because acquired and infused virtues, according to what has been said (A. 3), do not differ seemingly, save in relation to the last end. Now human habits and acts are specified, not by their last, but by their proximate end. Therefore the infused moral or intellectual virtue does not differ from the acquired virtue.

Obj. 2: Further, habits are known by their acts. But the act of infused and acquired temperance is the same, viz. to moderate desires of touch. Therefore they do not differ in species.

Obj. 3: Further, acquired and infused virtue differ as that which is wrought by God immediately, from that which is wrought by a creature. But the man whom God made, is of the same species as a man begotten naturally; and the eye which He gave to the man born blind, as one produced by the power of generation. Therefore it seems that acquired and infused virtue belong to the same species.

On the contrary, Any change introduced into the difference expressed in a definition involves a difference of species. But the definition of infused virtue contains the words, "which God works in us without us," as stated above (Q. 55, A. 4). Therefore acquired virtue, to which these words cannot apply, is not of the same species as infused virtue.

I answer that, There is a twofold specific difference among habits. The first, as stated above (Q. 54, A. 2; Q. 56, A. 2; Q. 60, A. 1), is taken from the specific and formal aspects of their objects. Now the object of every virtue is a good considered as in that virtue's proper matter: thus the object of temperance is a good in respect of the pleasures connected with the concupiscence of touch. The formal aspect of this object is from reason which fixes the mean in these concupiscences: while the material element is something on the part of the concupiscences. Now it is evident that the mean that is appointed in such like concupiscences according to the rule of human reason, is seen under a different aspect from the mean which is fixed according to Divine rule. For instance, in the consumption of food, the mean fixed by human reason, is that food should not harm the health of the body, nor hinder the use of reason: whereas, according to the Divine rule, it behooves man to "chastise his body, and bring it into subjection" (1 Cor. 9:27), by abstinence in food, drink and the like. It is therefore evident that infused and acquired temperance differ in species; and the same applies to the other virtues.

The other specific difference among habits is taken from the things to which they are directed: for a man's health and a horse's are not of the same species, on account of the difference between the natures to which their respective healths are directed. In the same sense, the Philosopher says (Polit. iii, 3) that citizens have diverse virtues according as they are well directed to diverse forms of government. In the same way, too, those infused moral virtues, whereby men behave well in respect of their being "fellow-citizens with the saints, and of the household [Douay: 'domestics'] of God" (Eph. 2:19), differ from the acquired virtues, whereby man behaves well in respect of human affairs.

Reply Obj. 1: Infused and acquired virtue differ not only in relation to the ultimate end, but also in relation to their proper objects, as stated.

Reply Obj. 2: Both acquired and infused temperance moderate desires for pleasures of touch, but for different reasons, as stated: wherefore their respective acts are not identical.

Reply Obj. 3: God gave the man born blind an eye for the same act as the act for which other eyes are formed naturally: consequently it was of the same species. It would be the same if God wished to give a man miraculously virtues, such as those that are acquired by acts. But the case is not so in the question before us, as stated.

On Law [Question 94]

Question 94

Of the Natural Law
(In Six Articles)

We must now consider the natural law; concerning which there are six points of inquiry:

(1) What is the natural law?
(2) What are the precepts of the natural law?
(3) Whether all acts of virtue are prescribed by the natural law?
(4) Whether the natural law is the same in all?
(5) Whether it is changeable?
(6) Whether it can be abolished from the heart of man?

First Article [I–II, Q. 94, Art. 1]

Whether the Natural Law Is a Habit?

Objection 1: It would seem that the natural law is a habit. Because, as the Philosopher says (Ethic. ii, 5), "there are three things in the soul: power, habit, and passion." But the natural law is not one of the soul's powers: nor is it one of the passions; as we may see by going through them one by one. Therefore the natural law is a habit.

Obj. 2: Further, Basil [*Damascene, De Fide Orth. iv, 22] says that the conscience or *synderesis* "is the law of our mind"; which can only apply to the natural law. But the "synderesis" is a habit, as was shown in the First Part (Q. 79, A. 12). Therefore the natural law is a habit.

Obj. 3: Further, the natural law abides in man always, as will be shown further on (A. 6). But man's reason, which the law regards, does not always think about the natural law. Therefore the natural law is not an act, but a habit.

On the contrary, Augustine says (De Bono Conjug. xxi) that "a habit is that whereby something is done when necessary." But such is not the natural law: since it is in infants and in the damned who cannot act by it. Therefore the natural law is not a habit.

I answer that, A thing may be called a habit in two ways. First, properly and essentially: and thus the natural law is not a habit. For it has been stated above (Q. 90, A. 1, ad 2) that the natural law is something appointed by reason, just as a proposition is a work of reason. Now that which a man does is not the same as that whereby he does it: for he makes a becoming speech by the habit of grammar. Since then a habit is that by which we act, a law cannot be a habit properly and essentially.

Secondly, the term habit may be applied to that which we hold by a habit: thus faith may mean that which we hold by faith. And accordingly, since the precepts of the natural law are sometimes considered by reason actually, while sometimes they are in the reason only habitually, in this way the natural law may be called a habit. Thus, in speculative matters, the indemonstrable principles are not the habit itself whereby we hold those principles, but are the principles the habit of which we possess.

Reply Obj. 1: The Philosopher proposes there to discover the genus of virtue; and since it is evident that virtue is a principle of action, he mentions only those things which are principles of human acts, viz. powers, habits and passions. But there are other things in the soul besides these three: there are acts; thus *to will* is in the one that wills; again, things known are in the knower; moreover its own natural properties are in the soul, such as immortality and the like.

Reply Obj. 2: *Synderesis* is said to be the law of our mind, because it is a habit containing the precepts of the natural law, which are the first principles of human actions.

Reply Obj. 3: This argument proves that the natural law is held habitually; and this is granted.

To the argument advanced in the contrary sense we reply that sometimes a man is unable to make use of that which is in him habitually, on account of some impediment: thus, on account of sleep, a man is unable to use the habit of science. In like manner, through the deficiency of his age, a child cannot use the habit of understanding of principles, or the natural law, which is in him habitually.

Second Article [I–II, Q. 94, Art. 2]

Whether the Natural Law Contains Several Precepts, or Only One?

Objection 1: It would seem that the natural law contains, not several precepts, but one only. For law is a kind of precept, as stated above (Q. 92, A. 2). If therefore there were many precepts of the natural law, it would follow that there are also many natural laws.

Obj. 2: Further, the natural law is consequent to human nature. But human nature, as a whole, is one; though, as to its parts, it is manifold. Therefore, either there is but one precept of the law of nature, on account of the unity of nature as a whole; or there are many, by reason of the number of parts of human nature. The result would be that even things relating to the inclination of the concupiscible faculty belong to the natural law.

Obj. 3: Further, law is something pertaining to reason, as stated above (Q. 90, A. 1). Now reason is but one in man. Therefore there is only one precept of the natural law.

On the contrary, The precepts of the natural law in man stand in relation to practical matters, as the first principles to matters of demonstration. But there are several first indemonstrable principles. Therefore there are also several precepts of the natural law.

I answer that, As stated above (Q. 91, A. 3), the precepts of the natural law are to the practical reason, what the first principles of demonstrations are to the speculative reason; because both are self-evident principles. Now a thing is said to be self-evident in two ways: first, in itself; secondly, in relation to us. Any proposition is said to be self-evident in itself, if its predicate is contained in the notion of the subject: although, to one who knows not the definition of the subject, it happens that such a proposition is not self-evident. For instance, this proposition, "Man is a rational being," is, in its very nature, self-evident, since who says "man," says "a rational being": and yet to one who knows not what a man is, this proposition is not self-evident. Hence it is that, as Boethius says (De Hebdom.), certain axioms or propositions are universally self-evident to all; and such are those propositions whose terms are known to all, as, "Every whole is greater than its part," and, "Things equal to one and the same are equal to one another." But some propositions are self-evident only to the wise, who understand the meaning of the terms of such propositions: thus to one who understands that an angel is not a body, it is self-evident that an angel is not circumscriptively in a place: but this is not evident to the unlearned, for they cannot grasp it.

Now a certain order is to be found in those things that are apprehended universally. For that which, before aught else, falls under apprehension, is *being*, the notion of which is included in all things whatsoever a man apprehends. Wherefore the first indemonstrable principle is that "the same thing cannot be affirmed and denied at the same time," which is based on the notion of *being* and *not-being*: and on this principle all others are based, as is stated in *Metaph.* iv, text. 9. Now as *being* is the first thing that falls under the apprehension simply, so *good* is the first thing that falls under the apprehension of the practical reason, which is directed to action: since every agent acts for an end under the aspect of good. Consequently the first principle of practical reason is one founded on the notion of good, viz. that "good is that which all things seek after." Hence this is the first precept of law, that "good is to be done and pursued, and evil is to be avoided." All other precepts of the natural law are based upon this: so that whatever the practical reason naturally apprehends as man's good (or evil) belongs to the precepts of the natural law as something to be done or avoided.

Since, however, good has the nature of an end, and evil, the nature of a contrary, hence it is that all those things to which man has a natural inclination, are naturally apprehended by reason as being good, and consequently as objects of pursuit, and their contraries as evil, and objects of avoidance. Wherefore according to the order of natural inclinations, is the order of the precepts of the natural law. Because in man there is first of all an inclination to good in accordance with the nature which he has in common with all substances: inasmuch as every substance seeks the preservation of its own being, according to its nature: and by reason of this inclination, whatever is a means of preserving human life, and of warding off its obstacles, belongs to the natural law. Secondly, there is in man an inclination to things that pertain to him more specially, according to that nature which he has in common with other animals: and in virtue of this inclination, those things are said to belong to the natural law, "which nature has taught to all animals" [*Pandect. Just. I, tit. i], such as sexual intercourse, education of offspring and so forth. Thirdly, there is in man an inclination to good, according to the nature of his reason, which nature is proper to him: thus man has a natural inclination to know the truth about God, and to live in society: and in this respect, whatever pertains to this inclination belongs to the natural law; for instance, to shun ignorance, to avoid offending those among whom one has to live, and other such things regarding the above inclination.

Reply Obj. 1: All these precepts of the law of nature have the character of one natural law, inasmuch as they flow from one first precept.

Reply Obj. 2: All the inclinations of any parts whatsoever of human nature, e.g. of the concupiscible and irascible parts, in so far as they are ruled by reason, belong to the natural law, and are reduced to one first precept, as stated above: so that the precepts of the natural law are many in themselves, but are based on one common foundation.

Reply Obj. 3: Although reason is one in itself, yet it directs all things regarding man; so that whatever can be ruled by reason, is contained under the law of reason.

Third Article [I–II, Q. 94, Art. 3]

Whether All Acts of Virtue Are Prescribed by the Natural Law?

Objection 1: It would seem that not all acts of virtue are prescribed by the natural law. Because, as stated above (Q. 90, A. 2) it is essential to a law that it be ordained to the common good. But some acts of virtue are ordained to the private good of the individual, as is evident especially in regards to acts of temperance. Therefore not all acts of virtue are the subject of natural law.

Obj. 2: Further, every sin is opposed to some virtuous act. If therefore all acts of virtue are prescribed by the natural law, it seems to follow that all sins are against nature: whereas this applies to certain special sins.

Obj. 3: Further, those things which are according to nature are common to all. But acts of virtue are not common to all: since a thing is virtuous in one, and vicious in another. Therefore not all acts of virtue are prescribed by the natural law.

On the contrary, Damascene says (De Fide Orth. iii, 4) that "virtues are natural." Therefore virtuous acts also are a subject of the natural law.

I answer that, We may speak of virtuous acts in two ways: first, under the aspect of virtuous; secondly, as such and such acts considered in their proper species. If then we speak of acts of virtue, considered as virtuous, thus all virtuous acts belong to the natural law. For it has been stated (A. 2) that to the natural law belongs everything to which a man is inclined according to his nature. Now each thing is inclined naturally to an operation that is suitable to it according to its form: thus fire is inclined to give heat. Wherefore, since the rational soul is the proper form of man, there is in every man a natural inclination to act according to reason: and this is to act according to virtue. Consequently, considered thus, all acts of virtue are prescribed by the natural law: since each one's reason naturally dictates to him to act virtuously. But if we speak of virtuous acts, considered in themselves, i.e. in their proper species, thus not all virtuous acts are prescribed by the natural law: for many things are done virtuously, to which nature does not incline at first; but which, through the inquiry of reason, have been found by men to be conducive to well-living.

Reply Obj. 1: Temperance is about the natural concupiscences of food, drink and sexual matters, which are indeed ordained to the natural common good, just as other matters of law are ordained to the moral common good.

Reply Obj. 2: By human nature we may mean either that which is proper to man—and in this sense all sins, as being against reason, are also against nature, as Damascene states (De Fide Orth. ii, 30): or we may mean that nature which is common to man and other animals; and in this sense, certain special sins are said to be against nature; thus contrary to sexual intercourse, which is natural to all animals, is unisexual lust, which has received the special name of the unnatural crime.

Reply Obj. 3: This argument considers acts in themselves. For it is owing to the various conditions of men, that certain acts are virtuous for some, as being proportionate and becoming to them, while they are vicious for others, as being out of proportion to them.

Fourth Article [I–II, Q. 94, Art. 4]

Whether the Natural Law Is the Same in All Men?

Objection 1: It would seem that the natural law is not the same in all. For it is stated in the Decretals (Dist. i) that "the natural law is that which is contained in the Law and the Gospel." But this is not common to all men; because, as it is written (Rom. 10:16), "all do not obey the gospel." Therefore the natural law is not the same in all men.

Obj. 2: Further, "Things which are according to the law are said to be just," as stated in *Ethic.* v. But it is stated in the same book that nothing is so universally just as not to be subject to change in regard to some men. Therefore even the natural law is not the same in all men.

Obj. 3: Further, as stated above (AA. 2, 3), to the natural law belongs everything to which a man is inclined according to his nature. Now different men are naturally inclined to different things; some to the desire of pleasures, others to the desire of honors, and other men to other things. Therefore there is not one natural law for all.

On the contrary, Isidore says (Etym. v, 4): "The natural law is common to all nations."

I answer that, As stated above (AA. 2, 3), to the natural law belong those things to which a man is inclined naturally: and among these it is proper to man to be inclined to act according to reason. Now the process of reason is from the common to the proper, as stated in *Phys.* i. The speculative reason, however, is differently situated in this matter, from the practical reason. For, since the speculative reason is busied chiefly with necessary things, which cannot be otherwise than they are, its proper conclusions, like the universal principles, contain the truth without fail. The practical reason, on the other hand, is busied with contingent matters, about which human actions are concerned: and consequently, although there is necessity in the general principles, the more we descend to matters of detail, the more frequently we encounter defects. Accordingly then in speculative matters truth is the same in all men, both as to principles and as to conclusions: although the truth is not known to all as regards the conclusions, but only as regards the principles which are called common notions. But in matters of action, truth or practical rectitude is not the same for all, as to matters of detail, but only as to the general principles: and where there is the same rectitude in matters of detail, it is not equally known to all.

It is therefore evident that, as regards the general principles whether of speculative or of practical reason, truth or rectitude is the same for all, and is equally known by all. As to the proper conclusions of the speculative reason, the truth is the same for all, but is not equally known to all: thus it is true for all that the three angles of a triangle are together equal to two right angles, although it is not known to all. But as to the proper conclusions of the practical reason, neither is the truth or rectitude the same for all, nor, where it is the same, is it equally known by all. Thus it is right and true for all to act according to reason: and from this principle it follows as a proper conclusion, that goods entrusted to another should be restored to their owner. Now this is true for the majority of cases: but it may happen in a particular case that it would be injurious, and therefore unreasonable, to restore goods held in trust; for instance, if they are claimed for the purpose of fighting against one's country. And this principle will be found to fail the more, according as we descend further into detail, e.g. if one were to say that goods held in trust should be restored with such and such a guarantee, or in such and such a way; because the greater the number of conditions added, the greater the number of ways in which the principle may fail, so that it be not right to restore or not to restore.

Consequently we must say that the natural law, as to general principles, is the same for all, both as to rectitude and as to knowledge. But as to certain matters of detail, which are conclusions, as it were, of those general principles, it is the same for all in the majority of cases, both as to rectitude and as to knowledge; and yet in some few cases it may fail, both as to rectitude, by reason of certain obstacles (just as natures subject to generation and corruption fail in some few cases on account of some obstacle), and as to knowledge, since in some the reason is perverted by passion, or evil habit, or an evil disposition of nature; thus formerly, theft, although it is expressly contrary to the natural law, was not considered wrong among the Germans, as Julius Caesar relates (De Bello Gall. vi).

Reply Obj. 1: The meaning of the sentence quoted is not that whatever is contained in the Law and the Gospel belongs to the natural law, since they contain many things that are above nature; but that whatever belongs to the natural law is fully contained in them. Wherefore Gratian, after saying that "the natural law is what is contained in the Law and the Gospel," adds at once, by way of example, "by which everyone is commanded to do to others as he would be done by."

Reply Obj. 2: The saying of the Philosopher is to be understood of things that are naturally just, not as general principles, but as conclusions drawn from them, having rectitude in the majority of cases, but failing in a few.

Reply Obj. 3: As, in man, reason rules and commands the other powers, so all the natural inclinations belonging to the other powers must needs be directed according to reason. Wherefore it is universally right for all men, that all their inclinations should be directed according to reason.

Fifth Article [I–II, Q. 94, Art. 5]

Whether the Natural Law Can Be Changed?

Objection 1: It would seem that the natural law can be changed. Because on Ecclus. 17:9, "He gave them instructions, and the law of life," the gloss says: "He wished the law of the letter to be written, in order to correct the law of nature." But that which is corrected is changed. Therefore the natural law can be changed.

Obj. 2: Further, the slaying of the innocent, adultery, and theft are against the natural law. But we find these things changed by God: as when God commanded Abraham to slay his innocent son (Gen. 22:2); and when he ordered the Jews to borrow and purloin the vessels of the Egyptians (Ex. 12:35); and when He commanded Osee to take to himself "a wife of fornications" (Osee 1:2). Therefore the natural law can be changed.

Obj. 3: Further, Isidore says (Etym. 5:4) that "the possession of all things in common, and universal freedom, are matters of natural law." But these things are seen to be changed by human laws. Therefore it seems that the natural law is subject to change.

On the contrary, It is said in the Decretals (Dist. v): "The natural law dates from the creation of the rational creature. It does not vary according to time, but remains unchangeable."

I answer that, A change in the natural law may be understood in two ways. First, by way of addition. In this sense nothing hinders the natural law from being changed: since many things for the benefit of human life have been added over and above the natural law, both by the Divine law and by human laws.

Secondly, a change in the natural law may be understood by way of subtraction, so that what previously was according to the natural law, ceases to be so. In this sense, the natural law is altogether unchangeable in its first principles: but in its secondary principles, which, as we have said (A. 4), are certain detailed proximate conclusions drawn from the first principles, the natural law is not changed so that what it prescribes be not right in most cases. But it may be changed in some particular cases of rare occurrence, through some special causes hindering the observance of such precepts, as stated above (A. 4).

Reply Obj. 1: The written law is said to be given for the correction of the natural law, either because it supplies what was wanting to the natural law; or because the natural law was perverted in the hearts of some men, as to certain matters, so that they esteemed those things good which are naturally evil; which perversion stood in need of correction.

Reply Obj. 2: All men alike, both guilty and innocent, die the death of nature: which death of nature is inflicted by the power of God on account of original sin, according to 1 Kings 2:6: "The Lord killeth and maketh alive." Consequently, by the command of God, death can be inflicted on any man, guilty or innocent, without any injustice whatever. In like manner adultery is intercourse with another's wife; who is allotted to him by the law emanating from God. Consequently intercourse with any woman, by the command of God, is neither adultery nor fornication. The same applies to theft, which is the taking of another's property. For whatever is taken by the command of God, to Whom all things belong, is not taken against the will of its owner, whereas it is in this that theft consists. Nor is it only in human things, that whatever is commanded by God is right; but also in natural things, whatever is done by God, is, in some way, natural, as stated in the First Part, Q. 105, A. 6, ad 1.

Reply Obj. 3: A thing is said to belong to the natural law in two ways. First, because nature inclines thereto: e.g. that one should not do harm to another. Secondly, because nature did not bring in the contrary: thus we might say that for man to be naked is of the natural law, because nature did not give him clothes, but art invented them. In this sense, "the possession of all things in common and universal freedom" are said to be of the natural law, because, to wit, the distinction of possessions and slavery were not brought in by nature, but devised by human reason for the benefit of human life. Accordingly the law of nature was not changed in this respect, except by addition.

Sixth Article [I–II, Q. 94, Art. 6]

Whether the Law of Nature Can Be Abolished from the Heart of Man?

Objection 1: It would seem that the natural law can be abolished from the heart of man. Because on Rom. 2:14, "When the Gentiles who have not the law," etc. a gloss says that "the law of righteousness, which sin had blotted out, is graven on the heart of man when he is restored by grace." But the law of righteousness is the law of nature. Therefore the law of nature can be blotted out.

Obj. 2: Further, the law of grace is more efficacious than the law of nature. But the law of grace is blotted out by sin. Much more therefore can the law of nature be blotted out.

Obj. 3: Further, that which is established by law is made just. But many things are enacted by men, which are contrary to the law of nature. Therefore the law of nature can be abolished from the heart of man.

On the contrary, Augustine says (Confess. ii): "Thy law is written in the hearts of men, which iniquity itself effaces not."

But the law which is written in men's hearts is the natural law. Therefore the natural law cannot be blotted out.

I answer that, As stated above (AA. 4, 5), there belong to the natural law, first, certain most general precepts, that are known to all; and secondly, certain secondary and more detailed precepts, which are, as it were, conclusions following closely from first principles. As to those general principles, the natural law, in the abstract, can nowise be blotted out from men's hearts. But it is blotted out in the case of a particular action, in so far as reason is hindered from applying the general principle to a particular point of practice, on account of concupiscence or some other passion, as stated above (Q. 77, A. 2). But as to the other, i.e. the secondary precepts, the natural law can be blotted out from the human heart, either by evil persuasions, just as in speculative matters errors occur in respect of necessary conclusions; or by vicious customs and corrupt habits, as among some men, theft, and even unnatural vices, as the Apostle states (Rom. i), were not esteemed sinful.

Reply Obj. 1: Sin blots out the law of nature in particular cases, not universally, except perchance in regard to the secondary precepts of the natural law, in the way stated above.

Reply Obj. 2: Although grace is more efficacious than nature, yet nature is more essential to man, and therefore more enduring.

Reply Obj. 3: This argument is true of the secondary precepts of the natural law, against which some legislators have framed certain enactments which are unjust.

III

Retrieving Aquinas
for Christian Life Today

The introduction of Aristotle into Europe and the entrance of theology into the new universities of the thirteenth century transformed the discipline in the West. Inculturation into the philosophical, scientific, and naturalistic thought of Aristotle changed theology into an inquiring and creative study. The logical methods and metaphysics of Aristotle, which Aquinas translated into categories of being, provided a deep ontological grounding for understanding the content of faith within a comprehensive framework of all reality. Aquinas helped to create a language for talking about grace and salvation that still works in a way analogous to how Newtonian physics still operates in a limited sphere despite the new physics of relativity and quantum mechanics. Newtonian physics put the first human being on the moon. In the last fifty years new telescopes and microscopes have revealed data that have once again transformed our understanding of the universe and the place of human beings in it. But reflection on the texts of Aquinas still releases relevant meaning for present-day spirituality. This retrieval of his language shows how faith and reason may be fused to stimulate a dynamic spirituality of action that also makes room for the mysticism of Eckhart.

Inculturation of Theology into the Universities

All are familiar with the issue of inculturation today because Christianity has become indigenized in so many non-Western cultures around the world. The same happens in intellectual culture, and theology should help the negotiation. Many historical and cultural factors came together, from trade and travel to architecture; these gave rise to larger towns and the urban universities. Aristotle, whom Aquinas sometimes simply referred to as "the philosopher," offered an integrated "secular" or naturalist worldview.[1] Internalizing Aristotle's deductive logic and his view of nature helped to enable and embolden a new inquisitive human spirit.

The deep structure of teleology, which Clement of Alexandria displayed a millennium before, took on a kind of deterministic quality in Aristotle's careful observations: every being possessed a nature and behaved accordingly. Aquinas had to understand Christian teachings about human existence, grace, virtue, and human behavior within the new naturalist vision of natures as principles of operation and action. In an Aristotelian world everything that exists has a nature or specific kind of being. Everything behaves according to its nature, so that nature, abilities, and kinds of behavior are lined up and point to their particular fulfillment or completion. All things are ordered in a teleological world and ends are achieved by the activities of beings over time. Aristotle's language expresses this order of things in what appears to be formal technical categories, but the content of his terms remain commonsensical: the nature of a being simply refers to the answer to the question, What is it? But the more or less consistent use of these set terms gave all who used them a new ability to ask questions and then answer them. This appears nowhere more clearly than in Thomas Aquinas's theology of grace.

Deep Metaphysical Framework for Christian Spirituality

The theology of grace deals with the foundational structure of Christian life. How one understands the working of grace determines how one understands God's interaction with human beings and the expected human response on the most fundamental level. Because the theology of grace reflects so profoundly a conception of the human relationship to God, it will become apparent that some of the major differences among Christian spiritualities have their roots here.[2] In the case of Aquinas, the keys to unlocking his vision lie, first, in the relation of grace to nature, where it was said that grace builds on and perfects nature. Then, second, the analogy between natural virtues and actions and supernatural virtues and actions immediately embeds spirituality in the theology of grace. Herein lies the basic structure of Aquinas's thought: he integrated what he learned of the Christian life from the tradition of the revelation of Jesus Christ and the natural system of an Aristotelian universe. Third, this carries over to a view of natural law that reflects the basic order of reality and can be perceived by everyone. But in the Christian dispensation human beings now follow the order of nature with supernatural motivation, empowerment by grace, shaped by faith, hope, and love, and leading to a supernatural goal called salvation or eternally shared life with God.

For all the talk about a Thomistic revolution in theology, however, his theology of grace and the spirituality it implied was both faithful to the theology of Augustine and well fitted to Western life in the towns of Christendom. Relative to Augustine, during the course of his conflict with Pelagius he formulated for Western theology a strong doctrine of original sin and the absolute priority of grace for each person's turning to God. This yielded a system in which Christian revelation infused human knowledge with transcendent and salvific insight. Grace, which Augustine equated with God as Spirit, infused human nature with God's loving assistance (*auxilium Dei*) to enable humans to attain salvation; grace overcame a debilitated or fallen human existence.

Aquinas preserved the Augustinian language: nature was "fallen" and needed "redemption." Saving grace was needed not only because of sin but also because of finitude and death. In Jesus Christ God calls human beings into a participation in God's own divine life. This entails God's saving grace that heals sin and guilt by forgiveness. The supernatural order of grace also refers to a final destiny of life with God that totally exceeds the powers of human nature. In the economy of grace, faith receives a new transforming kind of knowledge summarized in the Creed; and grace empowers nature to supernatural response, action, and fulfillment.

In Augustine, grace operated within the human person; in Thomas, grace functioned as a new human nature in a manner that raised the dynamics of knowing and willing to a new supernatural level. Human beings gained faith because God worked within and supported people in their assent of faith; human beings transcended sin in love of God and neighbor because God worked within them. Aquinas called the mechanism for this "habitual grace," a supernatural empowerment of the human spirit that allowed it, with God's help, to elicit the self-transcending actions that lead persons across their time to eternal salvation.

Ernst Troeltsch noticed how well the synthesis of Aquinas fit the cities and towns of Christendom.[3] The church was strongly established in much of Western Europe in the thirteenth century. Church and physical churches played a major role in common life. Divine grace was institutionally represented and delivered. The technical character of Aquinas's language of grace hides the precritical descriptive picture it called up for in the Medieval imagination. After baptism into Christian society, a person lived with God's gracious loving and forgiving presence within it. Persons only drove God out of their own lives by a serious conscious decision. This spirituality is distinctive in the way that it places God's grace within a person, but it was mediated by a church-in-society, so that one's whole life and especially one's actions were publicly supported in their intention, dynamism, and long-term goal. This framework provides strong support for a vocational spirituality in which one's way of life in society fits into a grand scheme of things and yet has particular value. Faith and baptism fit into a sphere of grace, therefore, and establishe one in a community whose members live on a grace-filled plane of existence. The Aristotelian world has been raised up to a higher supernatural sphere of life. Grace builds on nature, grace works within nature, and within the natural mechanisms of knowing and planning and acting. It thus transforms life into a dialogue of intimacy with God in response to God's grace. This was not a literate age of books, where one reads God's word in scripture; books were rare. But a world of grace was represented visually and audibly, on the walls outside and inside the churches, in the windows and up front on the altar and in the pulpit. Aquinas's theology of grace gave this mediation its metaphysical basis.

Dynamic Spirituality of Action

One of the problems with Aquinas's theology of grace lies in the fact that its analytical character distracts attention from its inner dynamism. His theology of grace explains divinely motivated human action and lays the groundwork for a spirituality of action. In the Jewish-Christian scriptures, the grounds for action lie in command and eschatology. One moves through time into the future by action. In Aquinas's theology, teleology, a cousin of eschatology, tends to coopt its temporality. When the two are held together, they deliver a dynamic spirituality of action across time that moves people toward their absolute future (eschatology), which corresponds with their purpose and goal (teleology). These metaphysical conceptions of things describe human life; life does not just exist but has a fundamental narrative character with an intended metaphysical plot. Human beings are created to know, love, and serve God through the way they act out their everyday lives until the end, when they reach their goal. As a metaphysical scheme, this pattern does not exclude people being in a personal and intimate relation with God along the way. In fact the narrative of grace describes fairly exactly what one saw in a medieval town, with a church in the center and perhaps a monastery nearby that provided the means and example of a nurtured, grace-filled supernatural life. One can find continuity here with life in the monastery, but the walls have been razed in this much more open structure that includes all of society.

Meister Eckhart (1260–1328) was a fellow Dominican who knew Aquinas's theology. He internalized Thomas Aquinas's conception of God as the absolutely transcendent pure act of being itself, so that all things that exist have their being because they participate in and share the power of being given them by God's immediate creating presence. In one of his sermons Meister Eckhart comments on the importance of human action for actual union with God, which is both the point of a Thomistic theology of grace and the point of spirituality itself. The sermon refers to the story of Mary and Martha (Luke 10:38–42) in which Mary sits at the feet of Jesus and listens to him speaking while Martha is busy preparing and carrying out the visit. Mary symbolizes contemplative life, Martha is the worker, and Eckhart uses them to represent the relation between "contemplation" and "action" in the Christian life.[4]

In his quirky interpretation of the story of Mary and Martha, seemingly opposite to what the text says, Eckhart shows the reversals that appear when one is personally and intimately united with God. Somewhat ironically for the mystic Eckhart, in Martha, the one "anxious" about many things, he found that God had produced the highest form of mystical union so that she "is able to work undisturbed in the midst of the concerns of the world."[5] He indicates how union with God overflows into action so that the summit of Christian spirituality is an active love of neighbor supported by "mysticism." Mary is still a learner and has not yet achieved an integration of contemplation and action.

Aquinas's theology of creation and grace working within a human being allows Eckhart to understand on a metaphysical level, perhaps also below reflective human consciousness, how union with God at this intimate level spontaneously overflows into action that goes out to others in a selfless way. At this mystical level, contemplation and action do not compete; action is completely infused by and flows out of an abiding union with God. No one in the Christian tradition has handled the relation between contemplation and action more deeply than Eckhart and his conclusions reflect a Thomistic theology of grace.

A spirituality of action is supported by a theology of cooperative grace. Augustine explicitly called attention to the idea of "cooperative grace" by differentiating it from God's initial or initiating grace, which is done "to" us and "in" us from outside, in the sense of beyond ourselves. Cooperative grace, however, is God's presence and power as Spirit sustaining our self-transcending actions. Much later in the medieval period Bernard of Clairvaux (1090–1153) showed that acts of true freedom under the influence of grace are completely human actions and at the same time completely done under the influence of grace. It was Thomas Aquinas, however, that most clearly showed why the simultaneous and complete authorship from two sources was possible: God's action is God's infinite creative presence, which cannot be understood as competing with human freedom. God's action, as creator and source of grace, sustains human freedom and cannot be imagined as a rival. In other words, the simplistic thought that God's grace opposes human freedom completely misses the point. In a spirituality of action God's grace is most operative when cooperating with human beings who are most free.[6]

This foundational medieval theology has been practically lost in many comparatively naïve controversies and conversations about human freedom within the sphere of grace. Too often religion itself and Christianity have been conceived as antithetical to human freedom. How often does the language of grace seem to be contrasted with what human freedom can accomplish? The whole Bible across its Testaments presupposes human freedom and initiative; it bears witness to a constant appeal to God for help and support of precisely the freedom and autonomy it takes for granted. But for many reasons people often use the common language of grace in a way that compromises and undermines freedom. In Augustine and Aquinas, the effect of grace is freedom that becomes real in action.

Ethics, Virtues, and the Spiritual Life

We turn now to the strong role that moral action plays in Aquinas's theology and to the essential role of ethics in spirituality. Aquinas laid out a fundamental teleological framework for understanding spirituality: a person's virtues, empowered by grace-filled human nature, enable human action to move toward life's goal of salvation. Why do humans exist? To praise and serve God and pass into eternal resurrected life. This formula, developed with minor variations, has governed Catholic spirituality since the High Middle Ages and is still operative today. Thomas Aquinas illustrates its intellectual rationale and aspects of its popular application. This appropriation of Aquinas's formula stays on the elementary schematic level in order to highlight the classical framework and to emphasize the central and positive role that morality plays in spiritual life. Only on that premise can we think about its weaknesses.

We saw in Aquinas's theology of grace the role that teleology plays in the adoption of Aristotelian language for theology. Jewish temporal, eschatological thinking was merged with a Greek metaphysical sense of goals and purpose very early in Christian thought, and Aquinas gave it an Aristotelian form. Salvation, which may be experienced in the moment, is not complete until the end of life; salvation is the goal of life, and life is a process leading to it. This metaphysical structure gives spirituality the status of a narrative. One's union with God, the essence of Christian spirituality, cannot be reduced to a state or a possession or a momentary vertical relationship; the relationship with God undergoes a historical journey toward final union. Time enters constitutively into the equation. Spirituality in Aquinas draws temporal historical life up into itself; spirituality is a temporal thing, a process. Union with God consists of an ongoing way of life in the sense that intentional living itself constitutes one's response and relation to God.

The dynamic temporal character of this understanding of spirituality opens up the formal question of the relation between the moral life and the spiritual life, between morality and spirituality. How should one formulate the close relationship between these two domains of human response without reducing one to the other? In this discussion, God's initiative of love prior to human response, God's grace, defines the source of union with God. But human freedom exercised in intentional action is in no way compromised by grace; grace protects human responsibility and morality. The premise for this discussion has to be anti-Pelagian: we do not save ourselves. But neither should we share the Augustinian view that, because it is gratuitous, grace is rare. It is impossible today to think of God's grace being withheld from some but not others by the creator. Also, Pelagius and Augustine share the view, each in his own way, that grace works within and through human freedom. But the question remains: how should we understand the whole secular sphere of morality, distinct from religious sensibility, and God's action in securing our union with God in relation to this moral sphere?

In the Thomistic system, virtues are the sources of good actions and the theological virtues lead to salvation. In other words, the theological virtues of faith, hope, and love are gifts of God given to human freedom and not self-generated. Therefore, the basis of this spirituality lies in grace, the effects of which appear as an internal impulse toward self-transcendence. Grace is God present and working within us. There can be no authentic Christian spirituality that is not based on God's gift of loving presence to us and acceptance of us. Spirituality cannot be reduced to morality.

At the same time both Augustine and Aquinas also called God's grace "cooperative," and there is no reason today why one should not think of God's grace as universally available to all human beings. This means that God's grace constantly solicits human freedom into action and carries it forward in response to God and God's will for human flourishing in the world. The power of grace engages human freedom and points its energy toward the good according to moral reasoning and responsibility at any given historical period and circumstance. In this view of things grace does not diminish the value of moral freedom and responsibility; it expands the metaphysical scope of freedom's inner intent and raises it up with salvific power to go where it could not go without grace. This does not change the basic structure of Augustine's and Aquinas's thinking. But it alters their suppositions, especially against Augustine who depicted the effective reach of God's love as limited. But, at the same time, using Augustinian and Thomistic reasoning, wherever one sees genuine altruistic concern for the other, one may presume that God's grace is cooperative.

In this scheme of things, virtues are "habits" or dispositions of our spirit or character that incline us to act in constructive ways; and theological virtues, like faith, hope, and altruistic love, channel the power of grace through intelligence and will into action according to what is perceived to be part of the ultimately good or of God's purpose. Since theological virtues are themselves products of grace, the actions they engender cannot be construed as self-salvation.[7] The deliberate ambiguity of the notion of cooperative grace does not undermine human responsibility or minimize the role of grace in a human life moving toward union with God and salvation. Freedom and grace do not compete in doing good; this is no zero-sum game. All moral behavior is supported by grace, and every moral act responds positively to the appeal of grace. Morality and spirituality are not the same thing. But one cannot have either one without the other.

It is safe to say that Thomistic theology, ethics, and spirituality to some degree contain the basic elements of the Catholic paradigm or framework for understanding the logic and dynamics of the Christian life. There is more to be said on that topic relative to the mediation of the church and sacraments, and we have not discussed Aquinas's social ethics. Also, all Christian theology in the Middle Ages did not follow Aquinas; some continued to cling to a purer form of Augustinian thinking. But in terms of a fundamental structure and pattern of reflection, Aquinas mediated a basic logic that underlies much of the catechetical formulations of the late Middle Ages. A good example of the influence of Aquinas comes from the opening sentence in Ignatius of Loyola's First Principle and Foundation in his Spiritual Exercises composed in the sixteenth century: "Human beings are created to praise, reverence, and serve God our Lord, and by means of this to save their souls."[8]

Conclusion: Negative and Positive Values

Thomas Aquinas's translation of his Augustinian convictions about God's saving grace into the language of Aristotle counts among the most controversial and far reaching of all his theological moves. God's grace is a reality; it is a kind of divine action that effects something within human beings. Because that effect is itself a form of being, it has a structure of being, a metaphysical ontology or kind of being. In a systematic theology that uses Aristotle's categories, Aquinas reflected upon and characterized the kind of being that grace is and how it governs, affects, and cooperates with natural human life, and how Christian human beings live under its influence. Almost as a matter of course, when this metaphysical (read speculative rather than physical) structure becomes spoken in common language, the whole system seems to become mechanistic. It did not take long before grace was used as a substantive, designating an entity, rather than a divine quality or affect influencing human soul or "form" of being. By the eve of the Reformation grace had become something that was able to be quantified in numbers that appear ridiculous today but made strange sense in another culture. In some measure this negative consequence is intrinsic to the language itself insofar as a person being sanctified by grace, losing it, and then regaining it again can be compared, in the Aristotelian system, to a physical change resulting in a new form of being. A glaring disparity separates the metaphysics of a physical "substantial change" and two subjects operating in an existential relationship of love.[9]

The slide away from a metaphysical imagination continues when morality becomes moralism and then legalism. The activist character of virtues in this spirituality gives rise to the idea of quantifying merit. This can be seen in countless documents and religious sermons that reduce Christian life to being good, not sinning or even making mistakes. So understood, the idea of being virtuous has lost its metaphysical depth of describing inner dispositions that add up to a holistic dimension of character. If this loss of depth combines with a legalist imagination, it conveys a spirituality of moral rectitude that tends to reduce Christian spirituality to a socially proper life: moralism. The extreme case that Luther saw happening in the sale of indulgences reduced spirituality to external behavior alone, without the faithful intentionality in which unity with God becomes actualized: spirituality becomes a kind of mechanical performance of certain actions. This can and has resulted in a view of life as a test before one enters one's true home that is not of this world. Suddenly Christian spirituality appears to be antihumanistic.

The positive side of this spirituality lies in its premise that grace is an acknowledged gift of God's presence within, which empowers rather than suppresses human freedom. Union with God is not compromised by the assumption of responsibility for moral action or by self-actualization. Union with God by grace stimulates action, so that moral responsibility is the very response that grace or the presence of God enables. Responsive human action does not go around grace but is empowered by grace. Cooperative grace sanctifies everyday activity, and intentional moral activity actualizes the power of grace when performance is channeled through theological and natural virtues. In this way God's grace becomes effective in history.

The following adjectives describe the medieval spirituality that emerged from Aquinas's theology of grace and his appropriation of Aristotle's virtue ethics: dynamic, narrative, moral, and grace filled. The dynamic character stems from the metaphysical framework that explains human nature as a potentiality for action toward a goal; in Christian spirituality this becomes movement toward final salvation in eternal life with the creator. Translated into the terms of time and history, the whole course of a person's life defined by the crises and decisions of everyday existence constitute this spirituality. The question of unity with God has both a present and a future dimension: do our actions lead in the direction of our eternal destiny? This spirituality places moral decision-making right in the center of human and thus spiritual life. But as Christian spirituality this agency recognizes that its relationship with God is grounded in God's creating and saving love or grace and not in an autonomous power of will over against God's agency.

Notes

1. Thomas Aquinas "thought it was the business of the natural sciences to trace this order of natural explanation (to show how the universe explains its own character). For this reason, he thought that there was no need for scientists to bring God into their scientific explanations. God is simply presupposed to be at the heart of the existence of the whole world that the scientist studies." Herbert McCabe, *Faith within Reason*, ed. Brian Davies (London: Continuum, 2007), 101.

2. This will be demonstrated in later volumes by Luther's reaction against Aristotelian theology, Calvin's characteristic differences from Luther, and Kant's providing a new philosophical base for Christian ethics and spirituality, and so on.

3. Ernst Troeltsch, *The Social Teaching of the Christian Churches* 1 (New York: Harper Torchbooks, 1960), 254–69.

4. Bernard McGinn, ed., *Meister Eckhart: Teacher and Preacher* (New York: Paulist Press, 1986), sermon 86.

5. Bernard McGinn, "Meister Eckhart: Mystical Teacher and Preacher," in *The Presence of God: A History of Western Christian Mysticism, IV, The Harvest of Mysticism in Medieval Germany (1300–1500)* (New York: Crossroad, 2005), 192.

6. These theologies are explained compactly in Roger Haight, *Faith and Evolution: A Grace-Filled Naturalism* (Maryknoll, NY: Orbis Books, 2019), 100–1, with references.

7. The very idea of "self-salvation" in an evolutionary world intrinsically marked by death seems like confused thinking.

8. Ignatius of Loyola, *The Spiritual Exercises of Saint Ignatius*, trans. and commentary George E. Ganss (Chicago: Loyola Press, 1992), #23.

9. This criticism is expanded in Roger Haight, *The Experience and Language of Grace* (New York: Paulist Press, 1979), 71–72.

Further Reading

Chenu, Marie-Dominique. *Toward Understanding Saint Thomas.* Chicago: Henry Regnery, 1964. (A French Dominican Medieval scholar retrieves the cultural and intellectual milieu of the universities of the thirteenth century and describes in detail the scholastic world in which Thomas Aquinas taught and wrote.)

Hütter Reinhard. *Dust Bound for Heaven: Explorations in the Theology of Thomas Aquinas.* Grand Rapids, MI: Eerdmans, 2012. (An expansive, sympathetic overview of the theological vision of Thomas Aquinas that recognizes Aquinas's Augustinianism and explicitly treats grace and the theological virtues.)

Kerr, Fergus. *Thomas Aquinas: A Very Short Introduction.* Oxford: Oxford University Press, 2009. (A short introduction to Thomas Aquinas by the well-known Irish Dominican theologian who surveys his life and works and gives an overview of the three parts of his *Summa Theologiae*.)

McCabe, Herbert. *On Aquinas.* Ed. Brian Davies. London, New York: Continuum, 2008. (A short book that focuses on human existence, written by a Dominican deeply influenced by Thomas Aquinas but also engaged in today's intellectual culture, bringing Thomas Aquinas to life for our time.)

Shields, Christopher, and Robert Pasnau. *The Philosophy of Aquinas.* New York: Oxford University Press, 2016. (Introduces the philosophy of Thomas Aquinas, which remains crucial for understanding his theology. Explicitly addresses the virtues and natural law in Aquinas.)

Torrell, Jean-Pierre. *Saint Thomas Aquinas. I. The Person and His Work*. Rev. ed. Washington, DC: Catholic University of America, 1996. (A full account of what we know of the life and work of Thomas Aquinas from a historical and biographical perspective.)

Turner, Denys. *Thomas Aquinas: A Portrait*. New Haven: Yale University Press, 2013. (Retrieves the author, Thomas Aquinas, from behind his philosophical and theological texts.)

About the Series

The volumes of this series provide readers direct access to important voices in the history of the faith. Each of the writings has been selected, first, for its value as a historical document that captures the cultural and theological expression of a figure's encounter with God. Second, as "classics," the primary materials witness to the "transcendent" in a way that has proved potent for the formation of Christian life and meaning beyond the particularities of the setting of its authorship.

Recent renewed interest in mysticism and spirituality have encouraged new movements, contributed to a growing body of therapeutic-moral literature, and inspired the recovery of ancient practices from Church tradition. However, the meaning of the notoriously slippery term "spirituality" remains contested. The many authors who write on the topic have different frameworks of reference, divergent criteria of evaluation, and competing senses of the principal sources or witnesses. This situation makes it important to state the operative definition used in this series. *Spirituality is the way people live in relation to what they consider to be ultimate.* So defined, spirituality is a universal phenomenon: everyone has one, whether they can fully articulate it or not. Spirituality emphasizes lived experience and concrete expression of one's principles, attitudes, and convictions, whether rooted in a

defined tradition or not. It includes not only interiority and
devotional practices but also the real outworkings of people's
ideas and values. Students of spirituality examine the way
that a person or group conceives of a meaningful existence
through the practices that orient them toward their horizon
of deepest meaning. What animates their life? What motivates
their truest desires? What sustains them and instructs them?
What provides for them a vision of the good life? How do
they define and pursue truth? And how do they imagine and
work to realize their shared vision of a good society?

The "classic" texts and authors presented in these volumes,
though they represent the diversity of Christian traditions,
define their ultimate value in God through Christ by the Spirit.
They share a conviction that the Divine has revealed God's
self in history through Jesus Christ. God's self-communication,
in turn, invites a response through faith to participate in an
intentional life of self-transcendence and to co-labor with
the Spirit in manifesting the reign of God. Thus, *Christian
spirituality refers to the way that individuals or social entities
live out their encounter with God in Jesus Christ by a life in
the Spirit.*

Christian spirituality necessarily involves a hermeneutical
task. Followers of Christ set about the work of integrating
knowledge and determining meaning through an interpreta-
tive process that refracts through different lenses: the life of
Jesus, the witness of the scripture, the norms of the faith
community, the traditions and social structures of one's
heritage, the questions of direct experience, the criteria of
the academy and other institutions that mediate truthfulness
and viability, and personal conscience. These seemingly competing authorities can leave contemporary students of theology with more quandaries than clarity. Thus, this series has
anticipated this challenge with an intentional structure that
will guide students through their encounter with classic texts.
Rather than providing commentary on the writings themselves, this series invites the audience to engage the texts with

an informed sense of the context of their authorship and a dialog with the text that begins a conversation about how to make the text meaningful for theology, spirituality, and ethics in the present.

Most of the readers of these texts will be familiar with critical historical methods which enable an understanding of scripture in the context within which it was written. However, many people read scripture according to the common sense understanding of their ordinary language. This almost inevitably leads to some degree of misinterpretation. The Bible's content lies embedded in its cultural context, which is foreign to the experience of contemporary believers. Critical historical study enables a reader to get closer to an authentic past meaning by explicitly attending to the historical period, the situation of the author, and other particularities of the composition of the text. For example, one would miss the point of the story of the "Good Samaritan" if one did not recognize that the first-century Palestinian conflict between Jews and Samaritans makes the hero of the Jewish parable an enemy and an unlikely model of virtue! Something deeper than a simple offer of neighborly love is going on in this text.

However, the more exacting the critical historical method becomes, the greater it increases the distance between the text and the present-day reader. Thus, a second obstacle to interpreting classics for contemporary theology, ethics, and spirituality lies in a bias that texts embedded in a world so different from today cannot carry an inner authority for present life. How can we find something both true and relevant for faith today in a witness that a critical historical method determines to be in some measure alien? The basic problem has two dimensions: how do we appreciate the past witnesses of our tradition on their own terms, and, once we have, how can we learn from something so dissimilar?

Most Christians have some experience navigating this dilemma through biblical interpretation. Through Church membership, Christians have gained familiarity with scriptural language, and preaching consistently applies its content to daily life. But beyond the Bible, a long history of cultural understanding, linguistic innovation, doctrinal negotiations, and shifting patterns of practices has added layer upon layer of meaning to Christian spirituality. Veiled in unfamiliar grammar, images, and politics, these texts may appear as cultural artifacts suitable only for scholarly treatments. How can a modern student of theology understand a text cloaked in an unknown history and still encounter in it a transcendent faith that animates life in the present? Many historical and theological aspects of Christian spirituality that are still operative in communities of faith are losing traction among swathes of the population, especially younger generations. Their premises have been called into question; the metaphors are dead; the symbols appear unable to mediate grace; and the ideas appear untenable. For example, is the human species really saved by the blood of Jesus on the cross? What does it mean to be resurrected from the dead? How does the Spirit unify if the church is so divided? On the other hand, the positive experiences and insights that accrued over time and added depth to Christian spirituality are being lost because they lack critical appropriation for our time. For example, has asceticism been completely lost in present-day spirituality or can we find meaning for it today? Do the mystics live in another universe, or can we find mystical dimensions in religious consciousness today? Does monasticism bear meaning for those who live outside the walls?

This series addresses these questions with a three-fold strategy. The historical first step introduces the reader to individuals who represent key ideas, themes, movements, doctrinal developments, or remarkable distinctions in theology, ethics, or spirituality. This first section will equip readers with a sense of the context of the authorship and a grammar for understanding the text.

Second, the reader will encounter the witnesses in their own words. The selected excerpts from the authors' works have exercised great influence in the history of Christianity. Letting these texts speak for themselves will enable readers to encounter the wisdom and insight of these classics anew. Equipped with the necessary background and language from the introduction, students of theology will bring the questions and concerns of their world into contact with the world of the authors. This move personalizes the objective historical context and allows the existential character of the classic witness to appear. The goal is not the study of the exact meaning of ancient texts, as important as that is. That would require a task outside the scope of this series. Recommended readings will be provided for those who wish to continue digging into this important part of interpretation. These classic texts are not presented as comprehensive representations of their authors but as statements of basic characteristic ideas that still have bearing on lived experience of faith in the twenty-first century. The emphasis lies on existential depth of meaning rather than adequate representation of an historical period which can be supplemented by other sources.

Finally, each volume also offers a preliminary interpretation of the relevance of the author and text for the present. The methodical interpretations seek to preserve the past historical meanings while also bringing them forward in a way that is relevant to life in a technologically developed and pluralistic secular culture. Each retrieval looks for those aspects that can open realistic possibilities for viable spiritual meaning in current lived experience. In the unfolding wisdom of the many volumes, many distinct aspects of the Christian history of spirituality converge into a fuller, deeper, more far-reaching, and resonant language that shows what in our time has been taken for granted, needs adjustment, or has been lost (or should be). The series begins with fifteen volumes but, like Cassian's *Conferences*, the list may grow.

About the Editors

ROGER HAIGHT is a visiting professor at Union Theological Seminary in New York. He has written several books in the area of fundamental theology. A graduate of the University of Chicago, he is a past president of the Catholic Theological Society of America.

ALFRED PACH III is an Associate Professor of Medical Sciences and Global Health at the Hackensack Meridian School of Medicine. He has a PhD from the University of Wisconsin in Madison and an MDiv in Psychology and Religion from Union Theological Seminary.

AMANDA AVILA KAMINSKI is an Assistant Professor of Theology at Texas Lutheran University, where she also leads the faith, diversity, and culture track in Social Innovation and Social Entrepreneurship. She has written extensively in this area of Christian spirituality.

Past Light on Present Life:
Theology, Ethics, and Spirituality

Roger Haight, SJ, Alfred Pach III,
and *Amanda Avila Kaminski,* series editors

Available titles: